Selected Writings from Mikhail Bakunin

by Mikhail Bakunin

Red and Black Publishers, St Petersburg, Florida

Library of Congress Cataloging-in-Publication Data

Bakunin, Mikhail Aleksandrovich, 1814-1876.
   [Selections. English. 2010]
   Selected writings from Mikhail Bakunin : by Mikhail Bakunin.
      p. cm.
   ISBN 978-1-934941-83-6
1. Socialism. 2. Freedom. 3. State, The. I. Title.
   HX914.7.B34A25 2010
   335'.83092--dc22

                                          2010007748

Red and Black Publishers, PO Box 7542, St Petersburg, Florida, 33734

Contact us at: info@RedandBlackPublishers.com

   Printed and manufactured in the United States of America

Contents

Editor's Preface

"The liberty of man consists solely in this, that he obeys the laws of nature because he has himself recognized them as such, and not because they have been imposed upon him externally by any foreign will whatsoever, human or divine, collective or individual." – Mikhail Bakunin

Mikhail Alexandrovich Bakunin was born in Russia in May 1814, the son of a Tsarist nobleman. He lived a life typical of the Russian aristocracy and joined the Tsarist Army as a junior officer, only to resign his commission and travel to university in Moscow to study philosophy, including Kant and Hegel. He was the first one to translate Fichte and Hegel's works into Russian.

Bakunin also came in contact with some of the many revolutionary groups that opposed the Tsar, and soon adopted their radical republican anti-Tsar and anti-religion programs. In 1842, Bakunin left Moscow and attended the University of Berlin, where he met a great number of German and Swiss radicals. By 1844 he was in Paris, where he met the anarchist Pierre-Joseph Proudhon and the socialist Karl Marx. He also began writing speeches and pamphlets condemning the Tsarist autocracy. Later that year, when word reached the Russian secret police of Bakunin's political activity, the Russian Tsar stripped Bakunin of his inherited noble titles, confiscated all his lands in Russia, and ordered his arrest.

As a result of diplomatic pressure by the Tsar, Bakunin was deported by the French government, and settled in Belgium. When the Revolutions of 1848 swept Europe, Bakunin tried to go to Poland but was stopped by German police, and went instead to Prague, where he helped organize an unsuccessful Pan-Slav rebellion to free eastern Europe from Russia. Returning to Germany, he began to publish pamphlets calling for the overthrow of the Prussian monarchy, and helped organize the uprising in Dresden in 1849. Arrested by German police, Bakunin was sentenced to death, but when the Tsarist government asked for his extradition, the German sentence was then commuted to life in prison and he was turned over to the Russians.

After being locked away for three years in the Peter and Paul Fortress, Bakunin was moved to the prison at Shlisselburg, where the conditions and diet were so bad that his teeth all fell out and he nearly died.

In 1857, after numerous pleas by Bakunin's aristocratic mother and father to the new Tsar, Alexander II, Bakunin was released from his cell and permanently exiled to the town of Tomsk in Siberia. Here he married the daughter of a Polish shopkeeper and, at the behest of General Count Muravyov, the Tsarist government official in charge of the area (who also happened to be Bakunin's second cousin), was allowed to move to the city of Irkutsk and given a job with the Amur Development Company. Irkutsk, the provincial capital of Siberia, was a place of political unrest, and contained a group of Siberian officials (including several of General Muravyov's own junior officers) who resented the colonial attitude taken towards them by the Tsar, and who advocated an independent nation of Siberia. Fearing that General Muravyov also had sympathies for a free Siberia, the Tsar replaced him with General Korsakov. Korsakov, as it happened, was also related to Bakunin by marriage.

Part of Bakunin's duties with the Amur Company required travel within the region, and in June 1861, General Korsakov provided him with papers giving him free passage on any ship on the Amur River, and granted him leave for a company trip to Nikolaevsk. In the port of Olga, however, Bakunin managed to talk his way aboard an American ship bound for Japan, and escaped Siberia, reaching Yokohama by August. Here, he happened to cross paths with Wilhelm Heine, a fellow radical who he had met before in Germany. Heine and Bakunin left Japan and arrived in San Francisco. From there, Bakunin booked passage to Panama, then to New York, and finally to England, where he arrived in December. His wife later emigrated from Russia and joined him.

For the next few years, he wrote for a number of radical newspapers. In 1863, he tried unsuccessfully to get to Poland, where revolt had broken out. Later that year, he went to Italy, where, in addition to meeting Garibaldi and Mazzini, he met a number of Italian anarchists, who had a profound impact on him. Up to this time, Bakunin had largely considered himself a republican and a socialist. Now he adopted anarchism. In his *Catechism of a Revolutionary*, written in 1866, he declared "absolute rejection of every authority including that which sacrifices freedom for the convenience of the state".

Back in England, Bakunin joined the League for Peace and Freedom, but his anarcho-socialist view was unpopular. A year later, the anarchists withdrew from the League and formed their own group, the Social Democratic Alliance.

In 1868, Bakunin met Karl Marx again and applied to have the Social Democratic Alliance join the International Workingmen's Association as a chapter. This was refused, on the grounds that IWA rules only allowed national groups to join, and the Alliance was international. In response, Bakunin broke up the Alliance and had its individual national chapters join IWA instead. The two factions, headed by Bakunin and Marx, soon became embroiled in a political debate that was to last the rest of their lives. While Bakunin accepted Marx's economic analysis of capitalism (he had been the first one to translate Marx's *Das Kapital* into Russian), he viewed any state, even the socialist one proposed by Marx, as an enemy, and declared that even a socialist state would inevitably descend into tyranny. "If you took the most ardent revolutionary and vested him in absolute power," Bakunin wrote, "within a year he would be worse than the Tsar himself."

In 1870, after the collapse of Louis Napoleon, Bakunin launched an unsuccessful uprising in Lyon. The next year, the Paris Commune roared to life, and, although the Commune was quickly crushed, both Bakunin and Marx claimed it as support for their own views on the revolutionary state.

In 1872, Bakunin's faction was expelled from the International, and set up its own anarchist International in Switzerland. Bakunin moved to Switzerland continued to write anarchist books and pamphlets, and tried to help organize a revolt in Italy, but was found by the police and forced to escape in disguise.

In 1876, faced with increasing health troubles, he entered a hospital in Berne, where he died in July.

God And The State

I.

Who are right, the idealists or the materialists? The question once stated in this way hesitation becomes impossible. Undoubtedly the idealists are wrong and the materialists right. Yes, facts are before ideas; yes, the ideal, as Proudhon said, is but a flower, whose root lies in the material conditions of existence. Yes, the whole history of humanity, intellectual and moral, political and social, is but a reflection of its economic history.

All branches of modem science, of true and disinterested science, concur in proclaiming this grand truth, fundamental and decisive: The social world, properly speaking, the human world—in short, humanity—is nothing other than the last and supreme development—at least on our planet and as far as we know—the highest manifestation of animality. But as every development necessarily implies a negation, that of its base or point of departure, humanity is at the same time and essentially the deliberate and gradual negation of the animal element in man; and it is precisely this negation, as rational as it is natural, and rational only because natural — at once historical and logical, as inevitable as the development and realization of all the natural laws in the world — that constitutes and creates the ideal, the world of intellectual and moral convictions, ideas.

Yes, our first ancestors, our Adams and our Eves, were, if not gorillas, very near relatives of gorillas, omnivorous, intelligent and ferocious beasts, endowed in a higher degree than the animals of another species with two precious faculties — the power to think and the desire to rebel.

These faculties, combining their progressive action in history, represent the essential factor, the negative power in the positive development of human animality, and create consequently all that constitutes humanity in man.

The Bible, which is a very interesting and here and there very profound book when considered as one of the oldest surviving manifestations of human wisdom and fancy, expresses this truth very naively in its myth of original sin. Jehovah, who of all the good gods adored by men was certainly the most jealous, the most vain, the most ferocious, the most unjust, the most bloodthirsty, the most despotic, and the most hostile to human dignity and liberty — Jehovah had just created Adam and Eve, to satisfy we know not what caprice; no doubt to while away his time, which must weigh heavy on his hands in his eternal egoistic solitude, or that he might have some new slaves. He generously placed at their disposal the whole earth, with all its fruits and animals, and set but a single limit to this complete enjoyment. He expressly forbade them from touching the fruit of the tree of knowledge. He wished, therefore, that man, destitute of all understanding of himself, should remain an eternal beast, ever on all-fours before the eternal God, his creator and his master. But here steps in Satan, the eternal rebel, the first freethinker and the emancipator of worlds. He makes man ashamed of his bestial ignorance and obedience; he emancipates him, stamps upon his brow the seal of liberty and humanity, in urging him to disobey and eat of the fruit of knowledge.

We know what followed. The good God, whose foresight, which is one of the divine faculties, should have warned him of what would happen, flew into a terrible and ridiculous rage; he cursed Satan, man, and the world created by himself, striking himself so to speak in his own creation, as children do when they get angry; and, not content with smiting our ancestors themselves, he cursed them in all the generations to come, innocent of the crime committed by their forefathers. Our Catholic and Protestant theologians look upon that as very profound and very just, precisely because it is monstrously iniquitous and absurd. Then, remembering that he was not only a God of vengeance and wrath, but also a God of love, after having tormented the existence of a few milliards of poor human beings and condemned them to an eternal hell, he took pity on the rest, and, to save them and reconcile his eternal and divine love with his eternal and divine anger, always greedy for victims and blood, he sent into the world, as an expiatory victim, his only son, that he might be killed by men. That is called the mystery of the Redemption, the basis of all the Christian religions. Still, if the divine Savior had saved the human world! But no; in the paradise promised by Christ, as we know, such being the formal announcement, the elect will number very few. The rest, the immense majority of the generations present and to come, will burn eternally in hell. In the meantime, to console us, God, ever just, ever good, hands over the earth to the government of the Napoleon Thirds, of the William Firsts, of the Ferdinands of Austria, and of the Alexanders of all the Russias.

Such are the absurd tales that are told and the monstrous doctrines that are taught, in the full light of the nineteenth century, in all the public schools of Europe, at the express command of the government. They call this civilizing the people! Is it not plain that all these governments are systematic poisoners, interested stupefies of the masses?

I have wandered from my subject, because anger gets hold of me whenever I think of the base and criminal means which they employ to keep the nations in perpetual slavery, undoubtedly that they may be the better able to fleece them. Of what consequence are the crimes of all the Tropmanns in the world compared with this crime of treason against humanity committed daily, in broad day, over the whole surface of the civilized world, by those who dare to call themselves the guardians and the fathers of the people? I return to the myth of original sin.

God admitted that Satan was right; he recognized that the devil did not deceive Adam and Eve in promising them knowledge and liberty as a reward for the act of disobedience which he bad induced them to commit; for, immediately they had eaten of the forbidden fruit, God himself said (see Bible): "Behold, the man is become as one of the gods, to know good and evil; prevent him, therefore, from eating of the fruit of eternal life, lest he become immortal like Ourselves."

Let us disregard now the fabulous portion of this myth and consider its true meaning, which is very clear. Man has emancipated himself; he has separated himself from animality and constituted himself a man; he has begun his distinctively human history and development by an act of disobedience and science — that is, by rebellion and by thought.

Three elements or, if you like, three fundamental principles constitute the essential conditions of all human development, collective or individual, in history: (1) human animality; (2) thought; and (3) rebellion. To the first properly corresponds social and private economy; to the second, science; to the third, liberty.

Idealists of all schools, aristocrats and bourgeois, theologians and metaphysicians, politicians and moralists, religionists, philosophers, or poets, not forgetting the liberal economists — unbounded worshippers of the ideal, as we know — are much offended when told that man, with his magnificent intelligence, his sublime ideas, and his boundless aspirations, is, like all else existing in the world, nothing but matter, only a product of vile matter.

We may answer that the matter of which materialists speak, matter spontaneously and eternally mobile, active, productive, matter chemically or organically determined and manifested by the properties or forces, mechanical, physical, animal, and intelligent, which necessarily belong to it—that this matter has nothing in common with the vile matter of the idealists. The latter, a product of their false abstraction, is indeed a stupid, inanimate, immobile thing, incapable of giving birth to the smallest product, a *caput mortuum*, an ugly fancy in contrast to the beautiful fancy which they call God; as the opposite of this supreme being, matter, their matter, stripped by that constitutes its real nature, necessarily represents supreme nothingness. They have taken away intelligence, life, all its determining qualities, active relations or forces, motion itself, without which matter would not even have weight, leaving it nothing but impenetrability and absolute immobility in space; they have attributed all these natural forces, properties, and manifestations to the imaginary being created by their abstract fancy; then, interchanging roles, they have called this product of their imagination, this phantom, this God who is nothing, "Supreme Being" and, as a necessary consequence, have declared that the real being, matter, the world, is nothing. After which they gravely tell us that this matter is incapable of producing anything, not even of setting itself in motion, and consequently must have been created by their God.

At the end of this book I exposed the fallacies and truly revolting absurdities to which one is inevitably led by this imagination of a God, let him be considered as a personal being, the creator and organizer of worlds; or even as impersonal, a kind of divine soul spread over the whole universe and constituting thus its eternal principle; or let him be an idea, infinite and divine, always present and active in the world, and always manifested by the totality of material and definite beings. Here I shall deal with one point only.

The gradual development of the material world, as well as of organic animal life and of the historically progressive intelligence of man, individually or socially, is perfectly conceivable. It is a wholly natural movement from the simple to the complex, from the lower to the higher, from the inferior to the superior; a movement in conformity with all our daily experiences, and consequently in conformity also with our natural logic, with the distinctive laws of our mind, which being formed and developed only by the aid of these same experiences; is, so to speak, but the mental, cerebral reproduction or reflected summary thereof.

The system of the idealists is quite the contrary of this. It is the reversal of all human experiences and of that universal and common good sense which is the essential condition of all human understanding, and which, in rising from the simple and unanimously recognized truth that twice two are four to the sublimest and most complex scientific considerations—admitting, moreover, nothing that has not stood the severest tests of experience or observation of things and facts—becomes the only serious basis of human knowledge.

Very far from pursuing the natural order from the lower to the higher, from the inferior to the superior, and from the relatively simple to the more complex; instead of wisely and rationally accompanying the progressive and real movement from the world called inorganic to the world organic, vegetables, animal, and then distinctively human—from chemical matter or chemical being to living matter or living being, and from living being to thinking being—the idealists, obsessed, blinded, and pushed on by the divine phantom which they have inherited from theology, take precisely the opposite course. They go from the higher to the lower, from the superior to the inferior, from the complex to the simple. They begin with God, either as a person or as divine substance or idea, and the first step that they take is a terrible fall from the sublime heights of the eternal ideal into the mire of the material world; from absolute perfection into absolute imperfection; from thought to being, or rather, from supreme being to nothing. When, how, and why the divine being, eternal, infinite, absolutely perfect, probably weary of himself, decided upon this desperate *salto mortale* is something which no idealist, no theologian, no metaphysician, no poet, has ever been able to understand himself or explain to the profane. All religions, past and present, and all the systems of transcendental philosophy, hinge on this unique and iniquitous mystery.

Holy men, inspired lawgivers, prophets, messiahs, have searched it for life, and found only torment and death. Like the ancient sphinx, it has devoured them, because they could not explain it. Great philosophers from Heraclitus and Plato down to Descartes, Spinoza: Leibnitz, Kant, Fichte, Schelling, and Hegel, not to mention the Indian philosophers, have written heaps of volumes and built systems as ingenious as sublime, in which they have said by the way many beautiful and grand things and discovered immortal truths, but they have left this mystery, the principal object of their transcendental investigations, as unfathomable as before. The gigantic efforts of the most wonderful geniuses that the world has known, and who, one after another, for at least thirty centuries, have undertaken anew this labor of Sisyphus, have resulted only in rendering this mystery still more incomprehensible. Is it to be hoped that it will be unveiled to us by the routine speculations of some pedantic disciple of an artificially warmed-over metaphysics at a time when all living and serious spirits have abandoned that ambiguous science born of a compromise — historically explicable no doubt — between the unreason of faith and sound scientific reason?

It is evident that this terrible mystery is inexplicable — that is, absurd, because only the absurd admits of no explanation. It is evident that whoever finds it essential to his happiness and life must renounce his reason, and return, if he can, to naive, blind, stupid faith, to repeat with Tertullianus and all sincere believers these words, which sum up the very quintessence of theology: *Credo quia absurdum* ("I believe because it is absurd"). Then all discussion ceases, and nothing remains but the triumphant stupidity of faith. But immediately there arises another question: How comes an intelligent and well-informed man ever to feel the need of believing in this mystery?

Nothing is more natural than that the belief in God, the creator, regulator, judge, master, curser, savior, and benefactor of the world, should still prevail among the people, especially in the rural districts, where it is more widespread than among the proletariat of the cities. The people, unfortunately, are still very ignorant, and are kept in ignorance by the systematic efforts of all the governments, who consider this ignorance, not without good reason, as one of the essential conditions of their own power. Weighted down by their daily labor, deprived of leisure, of intellectual intercourse, of reading, in short of all the means and a good portion of the stimulants that develop thought in men, the people generally accept religious traditions without criticism and in a lump. These traditions surround them from infancy in all the situations of life, and artificially sustained in their minds by a multitude of official poisoners of all sorts, priests and laymen, are transformed therein into a sort of mental and moral habit, too often more powerful even than their natural good sense.

There is another reason which explains and in some sort justifies the absurd beliefs of the people — namely, the wretched situation to which they find themselves fatally condemned by the economic organization of society in the most civilized countries of Europe. Reduced, intellectually and morally as well as materially, to the minimum of human existence, confined in their life like a prisoner in his prison, without horizon, without outlet, without even a future if we believe the economists, the people would have the singularly narrow souls and blunted instincts of the bourgeois if they did not feel a desire to escape; but of escape there are but three methods — two chimerical and a third real. The first two are the dram-shop and the church, debauchery of the body or debauchery of the mind; the third is social revolution. Hence I conclude this last will be much more potent than all the theological propagandism of the freethinkers to destroy to their last vestige the religious beliefs and dissolute habits of the people, beliefs and habits much more intimately connected than is generally supposed. In substituting for the at once illusory and brutal enjoyments of bodily and spiritual licentiousness the enjoyments, as refined as they are real, of humanity developed in each and all, the social revolution alone will have the power to close at the same time all the dram-shops and all the churches.

Till then the people, taken as a whole, will believe; and, if they have no reason to believe, they will have at least a right.

There is a class of people who, if they do not believe, must at least make a semblance of believing. This class comprising all the tormentors, all the oppressors, and all the exploiters of humanity; priests, monarchs, statesmen, soldiers, public and private financiers, officials of all sorts, policemen, gendarmes, jailers and executioners, monopolists, capitalists, tax-leeches, contractors and landlords, lawyers, economists, politicians of all shades, down to the smallest vendor of sweetmeats, all will repeat in unison those words of Voltaire:

"If God did not exist, it would be necessary to invent him." For, you understand, "the people must have a religion." That is the safety-valve.

There exists, finally, a somewhat numerous class of honest but timid souls who, too intelligent to take the Christian dogmas seriously, reject them in detail, but have neither the courage nor the strength nor the necessary resolution to summarily renounce them altogether. They abandon to your criticism all the special absurdities of religion, they turn up their noses at all the miracles, but they cling desperately to the principal absurdity; the source of all the others, to the miracle that explains and justifies all the other miracles, the existence of God. Their God is not the vigorous and powerful being, the brutally positive God of theology. It is a nebulous, diaphanous, illusory being that vanishes into nothing at the first attempt to grasp it; it is a mirage, an *ignis fatugs*; that neither warms nor illuminates. And yet they hold fast to it, and believe that, were it to disappear, all would disappear with it. They are uncertain, sickly souls, who have lost their reckoning in the present civilisation, belonging to neither the present nor the future, pale phantoms eternally suspended between heaven and earth, and occupying exactly the same position between the politics of the bourgeois and the Socialism of the proletariat. They have neither the power nor the wish nor the determination to follow out their thought, and they waste their time and pains in constantly endeavouring to reconcile the irreconcilable. In public life these are known as bourgeois Socialists.

With them, or against them, discussion is out of the question. They are too puny.

But there are a few illustrious men of whom no one will dare to speak without respect, and whose vigorous health, strength of mind, and good intention no one will dream of calling in question. I need only cite the names of Mazzini, Michelet, Quinet, John Stuart Mill. Generous and strong souls, great hearts, great minds, great writers, and the first the heroic and revolutionary regenerator of a great nation, they are all apostles of idealism and bitter despisers and adversaries of materialism, and consequently of Socialism also, in philosophy as well as in politics.

Against them, then, we must discuss this question.

First, let it be remarked that not one of the illustrious men I have just named nor any other idealistic thinker of any consequence in our day has given any attention to the logical side of this question properly speaking. Not one has tried to settle philosophically the possibility of the divine *salto mortale;* from the pure and eternal regions of spirit into the mire of the material world. Have they feared to approach this irreconcilable contradiction and despaired of solving it after the failures of the greatest geniuses of history, or have they looked upon it as already sufficiently well settled? That is their secret. The fact is that they have neglected the theoretical demonstration of the existence of a God, and have developed only its practical motives and consequences. They have treated it as a fact universally accepted, and, as such, no longer susceptible of any doubt whatever, for sole proof thereof limiting themselves to the establishment of the antiquity and this very universality of the belief in God.

This imposing unanimity, in the eyes of many illustrious men and writers—to quote only the most famous of them who eloquently expressed it, Joseph de Maistre and the great Italian patriot, Giuseppe Mazzini—is of more value than all the demonstrations of science; and if the reasoning of a small number of logical and even very powerful, but isolated, thinkers is against it, so much the worse, they say, for these thinkers and their logic, for universal consent, the general and primitive adoption of an idea has always been considered the most triumphant testimony to its truth. The sentiment of the whole world, a conviction that is found and maintained always and everywhere, cannot be mistaken; it must have its root in a necessity absolutely inherent in the very nature of man. And since it has been established that all peoples, past and present, have believed and still believe in the existence of God, it is clear that those who have the misfortune to doubt it, whatever the logic that led them to this doubt, are abnormal exceptions, monsters.

Thus, then, the antiquity; and universality; of a belief should be regarded, contrary to all science and all logic, as sufficient and unimpeachable proof of its truth. Why?

Until the days of Copernicus and Galileo everybody believed that the sun revolved about the earth. Was not everybody mistaken? What is more ancient and more universal than slavery? Cannibalism perhaps. From the origin of historic society down to the present day there has been always and everywhere exploitation of the compulsory labour of the masses—slaves, serfs, or wage workers—by some dominant minority; oppression of the people by the Church and by the State. Must it be concluded that this exploitation and this oppression are necessities absolutely inherent in the very existence of human society? These are examples which show that the argument of the champions of God proves nothing.

Nothing, in fact, is as universal or as ancient as the iniquitous and absurd; truth and justice, on the contrary, are the least universal, the youngest features in the development of human society. In this fact, too, lies the explanation of a constant historical phenomenon—namely, the persecution of which those who first proclaim the truth have been and continue to be the objects at the hands of the official, privileged, and interested representatives of "universal" and "ancient" beliefs, and often also at the hands of the same masses who, after having tortured them, always end by adopting their ideas and rendering them victorious.

To us materialists and Revolutionary Socialists, there is nothing astonishing or terrifying in this historical phenomenon. Strong in our conscience, in our love of truth at all hazards, in that passion for logic which of itself alone constitutes a great power and outside of which there is no thought; strong in our passion for justice and in our unshakeable faith in the triumph of humanity over all theoretical and practical bestialities; strong, finally, in the mutual confidence and support given each other by the few who share our convictions—we resign ourselves to all the consequences of this historical phenomenon, in which we see the manifestation of a social law as natural, as necessary, and as invariable as all the other laws which govern the world.

This law is a logical, inevitable consequence of the animal origin; of human society; for in face of all the scientific, physiological, psychological, and historical proofs accumulated at the present day, as well as in face of the exploits of the Germans conquering France, which now furnish so striking a demonstration thereof, it is no longer possible to really doubt this origin. But from the moment that this animal origin of man is accepted, all is explained. History then appears to us as the revolutionary negation, now slow, apathetic, sluggish, now passionate and powerful, of the past. It consists precisely in the progressive negation of the primitive animality of man by the development of his humanity. Man, a wild beast, cousin of the gorilla, has emerged from the profound darkness of animal instinct into the light of the mind, which explains in a wholly natural way all his past mistakes and partially consoles us for his present errors. He has gone out from animal slavery, and passing through divine slavery, a temporary condition between his animality and his humanity, he is now marching on to the conquest and realisation of human liberty. Whence it results that the antiquity of a belief, of an idea, far from proving anything in its favour, ought, on the contrary, to lead us to suspect it. For behind us is our animality and before us our humanity; human light, the only thing that can warm and enlighten us, the only thing that can emancipate us, give us dignity, freedom, and happiness, and realise fraternity among us, is never at the beginning, but, relatively to the epoch in which we live, always at the end of history. Let us, then, never look back, let us look ever forward; for forward is our sunlight, forward our salvation. If it is justifiable, and even useful and necessary, to turn back to study our past, it is only in order to establish what we have been and what we must no longer be, what we have believed and thought and what we must no longer believe or think, what we have done and what we must do nevermore.

So much for antiquity. As for the universality of an error, it proves but one thing — the similarity, if not the perfect identity, of human nature in all ages and under all skies. And, since it is established that all peoples, at all periods of their life, have believed and still believe in God, we must simply conclude that the divine idea, an outcome of ourselves, is an error historically necessary in the development of humanity, and ask why and how it was produced in history and why an immense majority of the human race still accept it as a truth.

Until we shall account to ourselves for the manner in which the idea of a supernatural or divine world was developed and had to be developed in the historical evolution of the human conscience, all our scientific conviction of its absurdity will be in vain; until then we shall never succeed in destroying it in the opinion of the majority, because we shall never be able to attack it in the very depths of the human being where it had birth. Condemned to a fruitless struggle, without issue and without end, we should for ever have to content ourselves with fighting it solely on the surface, in its innumerable manifestations, whose absurdity will be scarcely beaten down by the blows of common sense before it will reappear in a new form no less nonsensical. While the root of all the absurdities that torment the world, belief in God, remains intact, it will never fail to bring forth new offspring. Thus, at the present time, in certain sections of the highest society, Spiritualism tends to establish itself upon the ruins of Christianity.

It is not only in the interest of the masses, it is in that of the health of our own minds, that we should strive to understand the historic genesis, the succession of causes which developed and produced the idea of God in the consciousness of men. In vain shall we call and believe ourselves Atheists, until we comprehend these causes, for, until then, we shall always suffer ourselves to be more or less governed by the clamours of this universal conscience whose secret we have not discovered; and, considering the natural weakness of even the strongest individual against the all-powerful influence of the social surroundings that trammel him, we are always in danger of relapsing sooner or later, in one way or another, into the abyss of religious absurdity. Examples of these shameful conversions are frequent in society today.

II.

I have stated the chief practical reason of the power still exercised today over the masses by religious beliefs. These mystical tendencies do not signify in man so much an aberration of mind as a deep discontent at Heart. They are the instinctive and passionate protest of the human being against the narrowness, the platitudes, the sorrows, and the shame of a wretched existence. For this malady, I have already said, there is but one remedy—Social Revolution.

In the meantime I have endeavored to show the causes responsible for the birth and historical development of religious hallucinations in the human conscience. Here it is my purpose to treat this question of the existence of a God, or of the divine origin of the world and of man, solely from the standpoint of its moral and social utility, and I shall say only a few words, to better explain my thought, regarding the theoretical grounds of this belief.

All religions, with their gods, their demigods, and their prophets, their messiahs and their saints, were created by the credulous fancy of men who had not attained the full development and full possession of their faculties. Consequently, the religious heaven is nothing but a mirage in which man, exalted by ignorance and faith, discovers his own image, but enlarged and reversed—that is, divinized. The history of religion, of the birth, grandeur, and decline of the gods who have succeeded one another in human belief, is nothing, therefore, but the development of the collective intelligence and conscience of mankind. As fast as they discovered, in the course of their historically progressive advance, either in themselves or in external nature, a power, a quality, or even any great defect whatever, they attributed them to their gods, after having exaggerated and enlarged them beyond measure, after the manner of children, by an act of their religious fancy. Thanks to this modesty and pious generosity of believing and credulous men, heaven has grown rich with the spoils of the earth, and, by a necessary consequence, the richer heaven became, the more wretched became humanity and the earth. God once installed, he was naturally proclaimed the cause, reason, arbiter and absolute disposer of all things: the world thenceforth was nothing, God was all; and man, his real creator, after having unknowingly extracted him from the void, bowed down before him, worshipped him, and avowed himself his creature and his slave.

Christianity is precisely the religion par excellence, because it exhibits and manifests, to the fullest extent, the very nature and essence of every religious system, which is the impoverishment, enslavement, and annihilation of humanity for the benefit of divinity.

God being everything, the real world and man are nothing. God being truth, justice, goodness, beauty, power, and life, man is falsehood, iniquity, evil, ugliness, impotence, and death. God being master, man is the slave. Incapable of finding justice, truth, and eternal life by his own effort, he can attain them only through a divine revelation. But whoever says revelation says revealers, messiahs, prophets, priests, and legislators inspired by God himself; and these, once recognized as the representatives of divinity on earth, as the holy instructors of humanity, chosen by God himself to direct it in the path of salvation, necessarily exercise absolute power. All men owe them passive and unlimited obedience; for against the divine reason there is no human reason, and against the justice of God no terrestrial justice holds. Slaves of God, men must also be slaves of Church and State, in so far as the State is consecrated by the Church. This truth Christianity, better than all other religions that exist or have existed, understood, not excepting even the old Oriental religions, which included only distinct and privileged nations, while Christianity aspires to embrace entire humanity; and this truth Roman Catholicism, alone among all the Christian sects, has proclaimed and realized with rigorous logic. That is why Christianity is the absolute religion, the final religion; why the Apostolic and Roman Church is the only consistent, legitimate, and divine church.

With all due respect, then, to the metaphysicians and religious idealists, philosophers, politicians, or poets: The idea of God implies the abdication of human reason and justice; it is the most decisive negation of human liberty, and necessarily ends in the enslavement of mankind, both in theory and practice.

Unless, then, we desire the enslavement and degradation of mankind, as the Jesuits desire it, as the *mômiers*, pietists, or Protestant Methodists desire it, we may not, must not make the slightest concession either to the God of theology or to the God of metaphysics. He who, in this mystical alphabet, begins with A will inevitably end with Z; he who desires to worship God must harbor no childish illusions about the matter, but bravely renounce his liberty and humanity.

If God is, man is a slave; now, man can and must be free; then, God does not exist.

I defy anyone whomsoever to avoid this circle; now, therefore, let all choose.

Is it necessary to point out to what extent and in what manner religions debase and corrupt the people? They destroy their reason, the principal instrument of human emancipation, and reduce them to imbecility, the essential condition of their slavery. They dishonor human labor, and make it a sign and source of servitude. They kill the idea and sentiment of human justice, ever tipping the balance to the side of triumphant knaves, privileged objects of divine indulgence. They kill human pride and dignity, protecting only the cringing and humble. They stifle in the heart of nations every feeling of human fraternity, filling it with divine cruelty instead.

All religions are cruel, all founded on blood; for all rest principally on the idea of sacrifice — that is, on the perpetual immolation of humanity to the insatiable vengeance of divinity. In this bloody mystery man is always the victim, and the priest — a man also, but a man privileged by grace — is the divine executioner. That explains why the priests of all religions, the best, the most humane, the gentlest, almost always have at the bottom of their hearts — and, if not in their hearts, in their imaginations, in their minds (and we know the fearful influence of either on the hearts of men)—something cruel and sanguinary.

None know all this better than our illustrious contemporary idealists. They are learned men, who know history by heart; and, as they are at the same time living men, great souls penetrated with a sincere and profound love for the welfare of humanity, they have cursed and branded all these misdeeds, all these crimes of religion with an eloquence unparalleled. They reject with indignation all solidarity with the God of positive religions and with his representatives, past, present, and on earth.

The God whom they adore, or whom they think they adore, is distinguished from the real gods of history precisely in this— that he is not at all a positive god, defined in any way whatever, theologically or even metaphysically. He is neither the supreme being of Robespierre and J. J. Rousseau, nor the pantheistic god of Spinoza, nor even the at once immanent, transcendental, and very equivocal god of Hegel. They take good care not to give him any positive definition whatever, feeling very strongly that any definition would subject him to the dissolving power of criticism. They will not say whether be is a personal or impersonal god, whether he created or did not create the world; they will not even speak of his divine providence. All that might compromise him. They content themselves with saying "God" and nothing more. But, then, what is their God? Not even an idea; it is an aspiration.

It is the generic name of all that seems grand, good, beautiful, noble, human to them. But why, then, do they not say, "Man." Ah! because King William of Prussia and Napoleon III, and all their compeers are likewise men: which bothers them very much. Real humanity presents a mixture of all I that is most sublime and beautiful with all that is vilest and most monstrous in the world. How do they get over this? Why, they call one divine and the other bestial, representing divinity and animality as two poles, between which they place humanity.

They either will not or cannot understand that these three terms are really but one, and that to separate them is to destroy them.

They are not strong on logic, and one might say that they despise it. That is what distinguishes them from the pantheistical and deistical metaphysicians, and gives their ideas the character of a practical idealism, drawing its inspiration much less from the severe development of a thought than from the experiences, I might almost say the emotions, historical and collective as well as individual, of life. This gives their propaganda an appearance of wealth and vital power, but an appearance only; for life itself becomes sterile when paralyzed by a logical contradiction.

This contradiction lies here: they wish God, and they wish humanity. They persist in connecting two terms which, once separated, can come together again only to destroy each other. They say in a single breath: "God and the liberty of man," "God and the dignity, justice, equality, fraternity, prosperity of men" — regardless of the fatal logic by virtue of which, if God exists, all these things are condemned to non-existence. For, if God is, he is necessarily the eternal, supreme, absolute master, and, if such a master exists, man is a slave; now, if he is a slave, neither justice, nor equality, nor fraternity, nor prosperity are possible for him. In vain, flying in the face of good sense and all the teachings of history, do they represent their God as animated by the tenderest love of human liberty: a master, whoever he may be and however liberal he may desire to show himself, remains none the less always a master. His existence necessarily implies the slavery of all that is beneath him. Therefore, if God existed, only in one way could he serve human liberty — by ceasing to exist.

A jealous lover of human liberty, and deeming it the absolute condition of all that we admire and respect in humanity, I reverse the phrase of Voltaire, and say that, if God really existed, it would be necessary to abolish him.

The severe logic that dictates these words is far too evident to require a development of this argument. And it seems to me impossible that the illustrious men, whose names so celebrated and so justly respected I have cited, should not have been struck by it themselves, and should not have perceived the contradiction in which they involve themselves in speaking of God and human liberty at once. To have disregarded it, they must have considered this inconsistency or logical license practically necessary to humanity's well-being.

Perhaps, too, while speaking of liberty as something very respectable and very dear in their eyes, they give the term a meaning quite different from the conception entertained by us, materialists and Revolutionary Socialists. Indeed, they never speak of it without immediately adding another word, authority—a word and a thing which we detest with all our heart.

What is authority? Is it the inevitable power of the natural laws which manifest themselves in the necessary concatenation and succession of phenomena in the physical and social worlds? Indeed, against these laws revolt is not only forbidden—it is even impossible. We may misunderstand them or not know them at all, but we cannot disobey them; because they constitute the basis and fundamental conditions of our existence; they envelop us, penetrate us, regulate all our movements, thoughts, and acts; even when we believe that we disobey them, we only show their omnipotence.

Yes, we are absolutely the slaves of these laws. But in such slavery there is no humiliation, or, rather, it is not slavery at all. For slavery supposes an external master, a legislator outside of him whom he commands, while these laws are not outside of us; they are inherent in us; they constitute our being, our whole being, physically—intellectually, and morally: we live, we breathe, we act, we think, we wish only through these laws. Without them we are nothing, we are not. Whence, then, could we derive the power and the wish to rebel against them?

In his relation to natural laws but one liberty is possible to man—that of recognizing and applying them on an ever-extending scale in conformity with the object of collective and individual emancipation or humanization which he pursues. These laws, once recognized, exercise an authority which is never disputed by the mass of men. One must, for instance, be at bottom either a fool or a theologian or at least a metaphysician, jurist, or bourgeois economist to rebel against the law by which twice two make four. One must have faith to imagine that fire will not burn nor water drown, except, indeed, recourse be had to some subterfuge founded in its turn on some other natural law. But these revolts, or, rather, these attempts at or foolish fancies of an impossible revolt, are decidedly, the exception; for, in general, it may be said that the mass of men, in their daily lives, acknowledge the government of common sense—that is, of the sum of the natural laws generally recognized—in an almost absolute fashion.

The great misfortune is that a large number of natural laws, already established as such by science, remain unknown to the masses, thanks to the watchfulness of these tutelary governments that exist, as we know, only for the good of the people. There is another difficulty—namely, that the major portion of the natural laws connected with the development of human society, which are quite as necessary, invariable, fatal, as the laws that govern the physical world, have not been duly established and recognized by science itself.

Once they shall have been recognized by science, and then from science, by means of an extensive system of popular education and instruction, shall have passed into the consciousness of all, the question of liberty will be entirely solved. The most stubborn authorities must admit that then there will be no need either of political organization or direction or legislation, three things which, whether they emanate from the will of the sovereign or from the vote of a parliament elected by universal suffrage, and even should they conform to the system of natural laws—which has never been the case and never will be the case—are always equally fatal and hostile to the liberty of the masses from the very fact that they impose upon them a system of external and therefore despotic laws.

The liberty of man consists solely in this: that he obeys natural laws because he has himself recognized them as such, and not because they have been externally imposed upon him by any extrinsic will whatever, divine or human, collective or individual.

Suppose a learned academy, composed of the most illustrious representatives of science; suppose this academy charged with legislation for and the organization of society, and that, inspired only by the purest love of truth, it frames none but laws in absolute harmony with the latest discoveries of science. Well, I maintain, for my part, that such legislation and such organization would be a monstrosity, and that for two reasons: first, that human science is always and necessarily imperfect, and that, comparing what it has discovered with what remains to be discovered, we may say that it is still in its cradle. So that were we to try to force the practical life of men, collective as well as individual, into strict and exclusive conformity with the latest data of science, we should condemn society as well as individuals to suffer martyrdom on a bed of Procrustes, which would soon end by dislocating and stifling them, life ever remaining an infinitely greater thing than science.

The second reason is this: a society which should obey legislation emanating from a scientific academy, not because it understood itself the rational character of this legislation (in which case the existence of the academy would become useless), but because this legislation, emanating from the academy, was imposed in the name of a science which it venerated without comprehending—such a society would be a society, not of men, but of brutes. It would be a second edition of those missions in Paraguay which submitted so long to the government of the Jesuits. It would surely and rapidly descend to the lowest stage of idiocy.

But there is still a third reason which would render such a government impossible—namely that a scientific academy invested with a sovereignty, so to speak, absolute, even if it were composed of the most illustrious men, would infallibly and soon end in its own moral and intellectual corruption. Even today, with the few privileges allowed them, such is the history of all academies. The greatest scientific genius, from the moment that he becomes an academician, an officially licensed savant, inevitably lapses into sluggishness. He loses his spontaneity, his revolutionary hardihood, and that troublesome and savage energy characteristic of the grandest geniuses, ever called to destroy old tottering worlds and lay the foundations of new. He undoubtedly gains in politeness, in utilitarian and practical wisdom, what he loses in power of thought. In a word, he becomes corrupted.

It is the characteristic of privilege and of every privileged position to kill the mind and heart of men. The privileged man, whether politically or economically, is a man depraved in mind and heart. That is a social law which admits of no exception, and is as applicable to entire nations as to classes, corporations, and individuals. It is the law of equality, the supreme condition of liberty and humanity. The principal object of this treatise is precisely to demonstrate this truth in all the manifestations of human life.

A scientific body to which had been confided the government of society would soon end by devoting itself no longer to science at all, but to quite another affair; and that affair, as in the case of all established powers, would be its own eternal perpetuation by rendering the society confided to its care ever more stupid and consequently more in need of its government and direction.

But that which is true of scientific academies is also true of all constituent and legislative assemblies, even those chosen by universal suffrage. In the latter case they may renew their composition, it is true, but this does not prevent the formation in a few years' time of a body of politicians, privileged in fact though not in law, who, devoting themselves exclusively to the direction of the public affairs of a country, finally form a sort of political aristocracy or oligarchy. Witness the United States of America and Switzerland.

Consequently, no external legislation and no authority — one, for that matter, being inseparable from the other, and both tending to the servitude of society and the degradation of the legislators themselves.

Does it follow that I reject all authority? Far from me such a thought. In the matter of boots, I refer to the authority of the bootmaker; concerning houses, canals, or railroads, I consult that of the architect or engineer. For such or such special knowledge I apply to such or such a savant. But I allow neither the bootmaker nor the architect nor the savant to impose his authority upon me. I listen to them freely and with all the respect merited by their intelligence, their character, their knowledge, reserving always my incontestable right of criticism or censure. I do not content myself with consulting authority in any special branch; I consult several; I compare their opinions, and choose that which seems to me the soundest. But I recognize no infallible authority, even in special questions; consequently, whatever respect I may have for the honesty and the sincerity of such or such an individual, I have no absolute faith in any person. Such a faith would be fatal to my reason, to my liberty, and even to the success of my undertakings; it would immediately transform me into a stupid slave, an instrument of the will and interests of others.

If I bow before the authority of the specialists and avow my readiness to follow, to a certain extent and as long as may seem to me necessary, their indications and even their directions, it is because their authority is imposed upon me by no one, neither by men nor by God. Otherwise I would repel them with horror, and bid the devil take their counsels, their directions, and their services, certain that they would make me pay, by the loss of my liberty and self-respect, for such scraps of truth, wrapped in a multitude of lies, as they might give me.

I bow before the authority of special men because it is imposed upon me by my own reason. I am conscious of my inability to grasp, in all its details and positive developments, any very large portion of human knowledge. The greatest intelligence would not be equal to a comprehension of the whole. Thence results, for science as well as for industry, the necessity of the division and association of labor. I receive and I give—such is human life. Each directs and is directed in his turn. Therefore there is no fixed and constant authority, but a continual exchange of mutual, temporary, and, above all, voluntary authority and subordination.

This same reason forbids me, then, to recognize a fixed, constant, and universal authority, because there is no universal man, no man capable of grasping in that wealth of detail, without which the application of science to life is impossible, all the sciences, all the branches of social life. And if such universality could ever be realized in a single man, and if he wished to take advantage thereof to impose his authority upon us, it would be necessary to drive this man out of society, because his authority would inevitably reduce all the others to slavery and imbecility. I do not think that society ought to maltreat men of genius as it has done hitherto; but neither do I think it should indulge them too far, still less accord them any privileges or exclusive rights whatsoever; and that for three reasons: first, because it would often mistake a charlatan for a man of genius; second, because, through such a system of privileges, it might transform into a charlatan even a real man of genius, demoralize him, and degrade him; and, finally, because it would establish a master over itself.

To sum up. We recognize, then, the absolute authority of science, because the sole object of science is the mental reproduction, as well-considered and systematic as possible, of the natural laws inherent in the material, intellectual, and moral life of both the physical and the social worlds, these two worlds constituting, in fact, but one and the same natural world. Outside of this only legitimate authority, legitimate because rational and in harmony with human liberty, we declare all other authorities false, arbitrary and fatal.

We recognize the absolute authority of science, but we reject the infallibility and universality of the savant. In our church—if I may be permitted to use for a moment an expression which I so detest: Church and State are my two *bêtes noires*—in our church, as in the Protestant church, we have a chief, an invisible Christ, science; and, like the Protestants, more logical even than the Protestants, we will suffer neither pope, nor council, nor conclaves of infallible cardinals, nor bishops, nor even priests. Our Christ differs from the Protestant and Christian Christ in this—that the latter is a personal being, ours impersonal; the Christian Christ, already completed in an eternal past, presents himself as a perfect being, while the completion and perfection of our Christ, science, are ever in the future: which is equivalent to saying that they will never be realized. Therefore, in recognizing absolute science as the only absolute authority, we in no way compromise our liberty.

I mean by the words "absolute science," which would reproduce ideally, to its fullest extent and in all its infinite detail, the universe, the system or coordination of all the natural laws manifested by the incessant development of the world. It is evident that such a science, the sublime object of all the efforts of the human mind, will never be fully and absolutely realized. Our Christ, then, will remain eternally unfinished, which must considerably take down the pride of his licensed representatives among us. Against that God the Son in whose name they assume to impose upon us their insolent and pedantic authority, we appeal to God the Father, who is the real world, real life, of which he (the Son) is only a too imperfect expression, whilst we real beings, living, working, struggling, loving, aspiring, enjoying, and suffering, are its immediate representatives.

But, while rejecting the absolute, universal, and infallible authority of men of science, we willingly bow before the respectable, although relative, quite temporary, and very restricted authority of the representatives of special sciences, asking nothing better than to consult them by turns, and very grateful for such precious information as they may extend to us, on condition of their willingness to receive from us on occasions when, and concerning matters about which, we are more learned than they. In general, we ask nothing better than to see men endowed with great knowledge, great experience, great minds, and, above all, great hearts, exercise over us a natural and legitimate influence, freely accepted, and never imposed in the name of any official authority whatsoever, celestial or terrestrial. We accept all natural authorities and all influences of fact, but none of right; for every authority or every influence of right, officially imposed as such, becoming directly an oppression and a falsehood, would inevitably impose upon us, as I believe I have sufficiently shown, slavery and absurdity.

In a word, we reject all legislation, all authority, and all privileged, licensed, official, and legal influence, even though arising from universal suffrage, convinced that it can turn only to the advantage of a dominant minority of exploiters against the interests of the immense majority in subjection to them.

This is the sense in which we are really Anarchists.

The modern idealists understand authority in quite a different way. Although free from the traditional superstitions of all the existing positive religions, they nevertheless attach to this idea of authority a divine, an absolute meaning. This authority is not that of a truth miraculously revealed, nor that of a truth rigorously and scientifically demonstrated. They base it to a slight extent upon quasi-philosophical reasoning, and to a large extent also on sentiment, ideally, abstractly poetical. Their religion is, as it were, a last attempt to divinise all that constitutes humanity in men.

This is just the opposite of the work that we are doing. On behalf of human liberty, dignity and prosperity, we believe it our duty to recover from heaven the goods which it has stolen and return them to earth. They, on the contrary, endeavouring to commit a final religiously heroic larceny, would restore to heaven, that divine robber, finally unmasked, the grandest, finest and noblest of humanity's possessions. It is now the freethinker's turn to pillage heaven by their audacious piety and scientific analysis.

The idealists undoubtedly believe that human ideas and deeds, in order to exercise greater authority among men, must be invested with a divine sanction. How is this sanction manifested? Not by a miracle, as in the positive religions, but by the very grandeur of sanctity of the ideas and deeds: whatever is grand, whatever is beautiful, whatever is noble, whatever is just, is considered divine. In this new religious cult every man inspired by these ideas, by these deeds, becomes a priest, directly consecrated by God himself. And the proof? He needs none beyond the very grandeur of the ideas which he expresses and the deeds which he performs. These are so holy that they can have been inspired only by God.

Such, in so few words, is their whole philosophy: a philosophy of sentiments, not of real thoughts, a sort of metaphysical pietism. This seems harmless, but it is not so at all, and the very precise, very narrow and very barren doctrine hidden under the intangible vagueness of these poetic forms leads to the same disastrous results that all the positive religions lead to—namely, the most complete negation of human liberty and dignity.

To proclaim as divine all that is grand, just, noble, and beautiful in humanity is to tacitly admit that humanity of itself would have been unable to produce it—that is, that, abandoned to itself, its own nature is miserable, iniquitous, base, and ugly. Thus we come back to the essence of all religion—in other words, to the disparagement of humanity for the greater glory of divinity. And from the moment that the natural inferiority of man and his fundamental incapacity to rise by his own effort, unaided by any divine inspiration, to the comprehension of just and true ideas, are admitted, it becomes necessary to admit also all the theological, political, and social consequences of the positive religions. From the moment that God, the perfect and supreme being, is posited face to face with humanity, divine mediators, the elect, the inspired of God spring from the earth to enlighten, direct, and govern in his name the human race.

May we not suppose that all men are equally inspired by God? Then, surely, there is no further use for mediators. But this supposition is impossible, because it is too clearly contradicted by the facts. It would compel us to attribute to divine inspiration all the absurdities and errors which appear, and all the horrors, follies, base deeds, and cowardly actions which are committed, in the world. But perhaps, then, only a few men are divinely inspired, the great men of history, the virtuous geniuses, as the illustrious Italian citizen and prophet, Giuseppe Mazzini, called them. Immediately inspired by God himself and supported upon universal consent expressed by popular suffrage — *Dio e Popolo* — such as these should be called to the government of human societies.

But here we are again fallen back under the yoke of Church and State. It is true that in this new organization, indebted for its existence, like all the old political organisations, to the grace of God, but supported this time — at least so far as form is concerned, as a necessary concession to the spirit of modern times, and just as in the preambles of the imperial decrees of Napoleon III — on the (pretended) will of the people, the Church will no longer call itself Church; it will call itself School. What matters it? On the benches of this School will be seated not children only; there will be found the eternal minor, the pupil confessedly forever incompetent to pass his examinations, rise to the knowledge of his teachers, and dispense with their discipline — the people. The State will no longer call itself Monarchy; it will call itself Republic: but it will be none the less the State — that is, a tutelage officially and regularly established by a minority of competent men, men of virtuous genius or talent, who will watch and guide the conduct of this great, incorrigible, and terrible child, the people. The professors of the School and the functionaries of the State will call themselves republicans; but they will be none the less tutors, shepherds, and the people will remain what they have been hitherto from all eternity, a flock. Beware of shearers, for where there is a flock there necessarily must be shepherds also to shear and devour it.

The people, in this system, will be the perpetual scholar and pupil. In spite of its sovereignty, wholly fictitious, it will continue to serve as the instrument of thoughts, wills, and consequently interests not its own. Between this situation and what we call liberty, the only real liberty, there is an abyss. It will be the old oppression and old slavery under new forms; and where there is slavery there is misery, brutishness, real social materialism, among the privileged classes as well as among the masses.

In defying human things the idealists always end in the triumph of a brutal materialism. And this for a very simple reason: the divine evaporates and rises to its own country, heaven, while the brutal alone remains actually on earth.

Yes, the necessary consequence of theoretical idealism is practically the most brutal materialism; not, undoubtedly, among those who sincerely preach it — the usual result as far as they are concerned being that they are constrained to see all their efforts struck with sterility — but among those who try to realise their precepts in life, and in all society so far as it allows itself to be dominated by idealistic doctrines.

To demonstrate this general fact, which may appear strange at first, but which explains itself naturally enough upon further reflection, historical proofs are not lacking.

Compare the last two civilisations of the ancient world — the Greek and the Roman. Which is the most materialistic, the most natural, in its point of departure, and the most humanly ideal in its results? Undoubtedly the Greek civilisation. Which, on the contrary, is the most abstractly ideal in its point of departure — sacrificing the material liberty of the man to the ideal liberty of the citizen, represented by the abstraction of judicial law, and the natural development of human society to the abstraction of the State — and which became nevertheless the most brutal in its consequences? The Roman civilisation, certainly. It is true that the Greek civilisation, like all the ancient civilisations, including that of Rome, was exclusively national and based on slavery. But, in spite of these two immense defects, the former none the less conceived and realised the idea of humanity; it ennobled and really idealised the life of men; it transformed human herds into free associations of free men; it created through liberty the sciences, the arts, a poetry, an immortal philosophy, and the primary concepts of human respect. With political and social liberty, it created free thought. At the close of the Middle Ages, during the period of the Renaissance, the fact that some Greek emigrants brought a few of those immortal books into Italy sufficed to resuscitate life, liberty, thought, humanity, buried in the dark dungeon of Catholicism. Human emancipation, that is the name of the Greek civilisation. And the name of the Roman civilisation? Conquest, with all its brutal consequences. And its last word? The omnipotence of the Caesars. Which means the degradation and enslavement of nations and of men.

Today even, what is it that kills, what is it that crushes brutally, materially, in all European countries, liberty and humanity? It is the triumph of the Caesarian or Roman principle.

Compare now two modern civilisations — the Italian and the German. The first undoubtedly represents, in its general character, materialism; the second, on the contrary, represents idealism in its most abstract, most pure, and most transcendental form. Let us see what are the practical fruits of the one and the other.

Italy has already rendered immense services to the cause of human emancipation. She was the first to resuscitate and widely apply the principle of liberty in Europe, and to restore to humanity its titles to nobility: industry, commerce, poetry, the arts, the positive sciences, and free thought. Crushed since by three centuries of imperial and papal despotism, and dragged in the mud by her governing bourgeoisie, she reappears today, it is true, in a very degraded condition in comparison with what she once was. And yet how much she differs from Germany! In

Italy, in spite of this decline — temporary let us hope — one may live and breathe humanly, surrounded by a people which seems to be born for liberty. Italy, even bourgeois Italy, can point with pride to men like Mazzini and Garibaldi. In Germany one breathes the atmosphere of an immense political and social slavery, philosophically explained and accepted by a great people with deliberate resignation and free will. Her heroes — I speak always of present Germany, not of the Germany of the future; of aristocratic, bureaucratic, political and bourgeoisie Germany, not of the Germany of the *prolétaires* — her heroes are quite the opposite of Mazzini and Garibaldi: they are William I, that ferocious and ingenuous representative of the Protestant God, Messrs, Bismarck and Moltke, Generals Manteuffel and Werder. In all her international relations Germany, from the beginning of her existence, has been slowly, systematically invading, conquering, ever ready to extend her own voluntary enslavement into the territory of her neighbours; and, since her definitive establishment as a unitary power, she has become a menace, a danger to the liberty of entire Europe. Today Germany is servility brutal and triumphant.

To show how theoretical idealism incessantly and inevitably changes into practical materialism, one needs only to cite the example of all the Christian Churches, and, naturally, first of all, that of the Apostolic and Roman Church. What is there more sublime, in the ideal sense, more disinterested, more separate from all the interests of this earth, than the doctrine of Christ preached by that Church? And what is there more brutally materialistic than the constant practice of that same Church since the eighth century, from which dates her definitive establishment as a power? What has been and still is the principal object of all her contests with the sovereigns of Europe? Her temporal goods, her revenues first, and then her temporal power, her political privileges. We must do her the justice to acknowledge that she was the first to discover, in modern history, this incontestable but scarcely Christian truth that wealth and power, the economic exploitation and the political oppression of the masses, are the two inseparable terms of the reign of divine ideality on earth: wealth consolidating and augmenting power, power ever discovering and creating new sources of wealth, and both assuring, better than the martyrdom and faith of the apostles, better than divine grace, the success of the Christian propagandism. This is a historical truth, and the Protestant Churches do not fail to recognise it either. I speak, of course, of the independent churches of England, America, and Switzerland, not of the subjected churches of Germany. The latter have no initiative of their own; they do what their masters, their temporal sovereigns, who are at the same time their spiritual chieftains, order them to do, It is well known that the Protestant propagandism, especially in England and America, is very intimately connected with the propagandism of the material, commercial interests of those two great nations; and it is known also that the objects of the latter propagandism is not at all the enrichment and material prosperity of the countries into which it penetrates in company with the Word of God, but rather the exploitation of those countries with a view to the enrichment and material prosperity of certain classes, which in their own country are very covetous and very pious at the same time.

In a word, it is not at all difficult to prove, history in hand, that the Church, that all the Churches, Christian and non-Christian, by the side of their spiritualistic propagandism, and probably to accelerate and consolidate the success thereof, have never neglected to organise themselves into great corporations for the economic exploitation of the masses under the protection and with the direct and special blessing of some divinity or other; that all the States, which originally, as we know, with all their political and judicial institutions and their dominant and privileged classes have been only temporal branches of these various Churches have likewise had principally in view this same exploitation for the benefit of lay minorities indirectly sanctioned by the Church; finally and in general, that the action of the good God and of all the divine idealities on earth has ended at last, always and everywhere, in founding the prosperous materialism of the few over the fanatical and constantly famishing idealism of the masses.

We have a new proof of this in what we see today. With the exception of the great hearts and great minds whom I have before referred to as misled, who are today the most obstinate defenders of idealism? In the first places all the sovereign courts. In France, until lately, Napoleon III and his wife, Madame Eugénie; all their former ministers, courtiers, and ex-marshals, from Rouher and Bazaine to Fleury and Piétri; the men and women of this imperial world, who have so completely idealised and saved France; their journalists and their savants — the Cossagnacs, the Girardins, the Duvernois, the Veuillots, the Leverriers, the Dumas; the black phalanx of Jesuits and Jesuitesses in every garb; the whole upper and middle bourgeoisie of France; the doctrinaire liberals, and the liberals without doctrine — the Guizots, the Thiers, the Jules Favres, the Pelletans, and the Jules Simons, all obstinate defenders of the bourgeoisie exploitation. In Prussia, in Germany, William I, the present royal demonstrator of the good God on earth; all his generals, all his officers, Pomeranian and other; all his army, which, strong in its religious faith, has just conquered France in that ideal way we know so well. In Russia, the Czar and his court; the Mouravieffs and the Bergs, all the butchers and pious proselyters of Poland. Everywhere, in short, religious or philosophical idealism, the one being but the more or less free translation of the other, serves today as the flag of material, bloody, and brutal force, of shameless material exploitation; while, on the contrary, the flag of theoretical materialism, the red flag of economic equality and social justice, is raised by the practical idealism of the oppressed and famishing masses, tending to realise the greatest liberty and the human right of each in the fraternity of all men on the earth.

Who are the real idealists — the idealists not of abstraction, but of life, not of heaven, but of earth — and who are the materialists?

It is evident that the essential condition of theoretical or divine idealism is the sacrifice of logic, of human reason, the renunciation of science. We see, further, that in defending the doctrines of idealism one finds himself enlisted perforce in the ranks of the oppressors and exploiters of the masses. These are two great reasons which, it would seem, should be sufficient to drive every great mind, every great heart, from idealism. How does it happen that our illustrious contemporary idealists, who certainly lack neither mind, nor heart, nor good will, and who have devoted their entire existence to the service of humanity — how does it happen that they persist in remaining among the representatives of a doctrine henceforth condemned and dishonoured?

They must be influenced by a very powerful motive. It cannot be logic or science, since logic and science have pronounced their verdict against the idealistic doctrine. No more can it be personal interests, since these men are infinitely above everything of that sort. It must, then, be a powerful moral motive. Which? There can be but one. These illustrious men think, no doubt, that idealistic theories or beliefs are essentially necessary to the moral dignity and grandeur of man, and that materialistic theories, on the contrary, reduce him to the level of the beasts.

And if the truth were just the opposite?

Every development, I have said, implies the negation of its point of departure. The basis or point of departure, according to the materialistic school, being material, the negation must be necessarily ideal. Starting from the totality of the real world, or from what is abstractly called matter, it logically arrives at the real idealisation — that is, at the humanisation, at the full and complete emancipation of society. Per contra; and for the same reason, the basis and point of departure of the idealistic school being ideal, it arrives necessarily at the materialisation of society, at the organization of a brutal despotism and an iniquitous and ignoble exploitation, under the form of Church and State. The historical development of man according to the materialistic school, is a progressive ascension; in the idealistic system it can be nothing but a continuous fall.

Whatever human question we may desire to consider, we always find this same essential contradiction between the two schools. Thus, as I have already observed, materialism starts from animality to establish humanity; idealism starts from divinity to establish slavery and condemn the masses to an endless animality. Materialism denies free will and ends in the establishment of liberty; idealism, in the name of human dignity, proclaims free will, and on the ruins of every liberty founds authority. Materialism rejects the principle of authority, because it rightly considers it as the corollary of animality, and because, on the contrary, the triumph of humanity, the object and chief significance of history, can be realised only through liberty. In a word, you will always find the idealists in the very act of practical materialism, while you will see the materialists pursuing and realising the most grandly ideal aspirations and thoughts.

History, in the system of the idealists, as I have said, can be nothing but a continuous fall. They begin by a terrible fall, from which they never recover — by the *salto mortale*; from the sublime regions of pure and absolute idea into matter. And into what kind of matter! Not into the matter which is eternally active and mobile, full of properties and forces, of life and intelligence, as we see it in the real world; but into abstract matter, impoverished and reduced to absolute misery by the regular looting of these Prussians of thought, the theologians and metaphysicians, who have stripped it of everything to give everything to their emperor, to their God; into the matter which, deprived of all action and movement of its own, represents, in opposition to the divine idea, nothing but absolute stupidity, impenetrability, inertia and immobility.

The fall is so terrible that divinity, the divine person or idea, is flattened out, loses consciousness of itself, and never more recovers it. And in this desperate situation it is still forced to work miracles ! For from the moment that matter becomes inert, every movement that takes place in the world, even the most material, is a miracle, can result only from a providential intervention, from the action of God upon matter. And there this poor Divinity, degraded and half annihilated by its fall, lies some thousands of centuries in this swoon, then awakens slowly, in vain endeavouring to grasp some vague memory of itself, and every move that it makes in this direction upon matter becomes a creation, a new formation, a new miracle. In this way it passes through all degrees of materiality and bestiality — first, gas, simple or compound chemical substance, mineral, it then spreads over the earth as vegetable and animal organization till it concentrates itself in man. Here it would seem as if it must become itself again, for it lights in every human being an angelic spark, a particle of its own divine being, the immortal soul.

How did it manage to lodge a thing absolutely immaterial in a thing absolutely material; how can the body contain, enclose, limit, paralyse pure spirit? This, again, is one of those questions which faith alone, that passionate and stupid affirmation of the absurd, can solve. It is the greatest of miracles. Here, however, we have only to establish the effects, the practical consequences of this miracle.

After thousands of centuries of vain efforts to come back to itself, Divinity, lost and scattered in the matter which it animates and sets in motion, finds a point of support, a sort of focus for self-concentration. This focus is man, his immortal soul singularly imprisoned in a mortal body. But each man considered individually is infinitely too limited, too small, to enclose the divine immensity; it can contain only a very small particle, immortal like the whole, but infinitely smaller than the whole. It follows that the divine being, the absolutely immaterial being, mind, is divisible like matter. Another mystery whose solution must be left to faith.

If God entire could find lodgment in each man, then each man would be God. We should have an immense quantity of Gods, each limited by all the others and yet none the less infinite—a contradiction which would imply a mutual destruction of men, an impossibility of the existence of more than one. As for the particles, that is another matter; nothing more rational, indeed, than that one particle should be limited by another and be smaller than the whole. Only, here another contradiction confronts us. To be limited, to be greater and smaller are attributes of matter, not of mind. According to the materialists, it is true, mind is only the working of the wholly material organism of man, and the greatness or smallness of mind depends absolutely on the greater or less material perfection of the human organism. But these same attributes of relative limitation and grandeur cannot be attributed to mind as the idealists conceive it, absolutely immaterial mind, mind existing independent of matter. There can be neither greater nor smaller nor any limit among minds, for there is only one mind—God. To add that the infinitely small and limited particles which constitute human souls are at the same time immortal is to carry the contradiction to a climax. But this is a question of faith. Let us pass on.

Here then we have Divinity torn up and lodged, in infinitely small particles, in an immense number of beings of all sexes, ages, races, and colours. This is an excessively inconvenient and unhappy situation, for the divine particles are so little acquainted with each other at the outset of their human existence that they begin by devouring each other. Moreover, in the midst of this state of barbarism and wholly animal brutality, these divine particles, human souls, retain as it were a vague remembrance of their primitive divinity, and are irresistibly drawn towards their whole; they seek each other, they seek their whole. It is Divinity itself, scattered and lost in the natural world, which looks for itself in men, and it is so demolished by this multitude of human prisons in which it finds itself strewn, that, in looking for itself, it commits folly after folly.

Beginning with fetishism, it searches for and adores itself, now in a stone, now in a piece of wood, now in a rag. It is quite likely that it would never have succeeded in getting out of the rag, if the other divinity which was not allowed to fall into matter and which is kept in a state of pure spirit in the sublime heights of the absolute ideal, or in the celestial regions, had not had pity on it.

Here is a new mystery—that of Divinity dividing itself into two halves, both equally infinite, of which one—God the Father—stays in the purely immaterial regions, and the other—God the Son—falls into matter. We shall see directly, between these two Divinities separated from each other, continuous relations established, from above to below and from below to above; and these relations, considered as a single eternal and constant act, will constitute the Holy Ghost. Such, in its veritable theological and metaphysical meaning, is the great, the terrible mystery of the Christian Trinity.

But let us lose no time in abandoning these heights to see what is going on upon earth.

God the Father, seeing from the height of his eternal splendour that the poor God the Son, flattened out and astounded by his fall, is so plunged and lost in matter that even having reached human state he has not yet recovered himself, decides to come to his aid. From this immense number of particles at once immortal, divine, and infinitely small, in which God the Son has disseminated himself so thoroughly that he does not know himself, God the Father chooses those most pleasing to him, picks his inspired persons, his prophets, his "men of virtuous genius," the great benefactors and legislators of humanity: Zoroaster, Buddha, Moses, Confucius, Lycurgus, Solon, Socrates, the divine Plato, and above all Jesus Christ, the complete realisation of God the Son, at last collected and concentrated in a single human person; all the apostles, Saint Peter, Saint Paul, Saint John before all, Constantine the Great, Mahomet, then Charlemagne, Gregory VII, Dante, and, according to some, Luther also, Voltaire and Rousseau, Robespierre and Danton, and many other great and holy historical personages, all of whose names it is impossible to recapitulate, but among whom I, as a Russian, beg that Saint Nicholas may not be forgotten.

Then we have reached at last the manifestation of God upon earth. But immediately God appears, man is reduced to nothing. It will be said that he is not reduced to nothing, since he is himself a particle of God. Pardon me! I admit that a particle of a definite, limited whole, however small it be, is a quantity, a positive greatness. But a particle of the infinitely great, compared with it, is necessarily infinitely small. Multiply milliards of milliards by milliards of milliards—their product compared to the infinitely great, will be infinitely small, and the infinitely small is equal to zero. God is everything; therefore man and all the real world with him, the universe, are nothing. You will not escape this conclusion.

God appears, man is reduced to nothing; and the greater Divinity becomes, the more miserable becomes humanity. That is the history of all religions; that is the effect of all the divine inspirations and legislations. In history the name of God is the terrible club with which all divinely inspired men, the great "virtuous geniuses," have beaten down the liberty, dignity, reason, and prosperity of man.

We had first the fall of God. Now we have a fall which interests us more—that of man, caused solely by the apparition of God manifested on earth.

See in how profound an error our dear and illustrious idealists find themselves. In talking to us of God they purpose, they desire, to elevate us, emancipate us, ennoble us, and, on the contrary, they crush and degrade us. With the name of God they imagine that they can establish fraternity among men, and, on the contrary, they create pride, contempt; they sow discord, hatred, war; they establish slavery. For with God come the different degrees of divine inspiration; humanity is divided into men highly inspired, less inspired, uninspired. All are equally insignificant before God, it is true; but, compared with each other, some are greater than others; not only in fact—which would be of no consequence, because inequality in fact is lost in the collectivity when it cannot cling to some legal fiction or institution—but by the divine right of inspiration, which immediately establishes a fixed, constant, petrifying inequality. The highly inspired must be listened to and obeyed by the less inspired, and the less inspired by the uninspired. Thus we have the principle of authority well established, and with it the two fundamental institutions of slavery: Church and State.

Of all despotisms that of the doctrinaires, or inspired religionists, is the worst. They are so jealous of the glory of their God and of the triumph of their idea that they have no heart left for the liberty or the dignity or even the sufferings of living men, of real men. Divine zeal, preoccupation with the idea, finally dry up the tenderest souls, the most compassionate hearts, the sources of human love. Considering all that is, all that happens in the world, from the point of view of eternity or of the abstract idea, they treat passing matters with disdain; but the whole life of real men, of men of flesh and bone, is composed only of passing matters; they themselves are only passing beings, who, once passed, are replaced by others likewise passing, but never to return in person. Alone permanent or relatively eternal in men is humanity, which steadily developing, grows richer in passing from one generation to another. I say relatively eternal, because, our planet once destroyed—it cannot fail to perish sooner or later, since everything which has begun must necessarily end—our planet once decomposed, to serve undoubtedly as an element of some new formation in the system of the universe, which alone is really eternal, who knows what will become of our whole human development? Nevertheless, the moment of this dissolution being an enormous distance in the future, we may properly consider humanity, relatively to the short duration of human life, as eternal. But this very fact of progressive humanity is real and living only through its manifestations at definite times, in definite places, in really living men, and not through its general idea.

The general idea is always an abstraction and, for that very reason, in some sort a negation of real life. I have stated in the Appendix that human thought and, in consequence of this, science can grasp and name only the general significance of real facts, their relations, their laws—in short, that which is permanent in their continual transformations—but never their material, individual side, palpitating, so to speak, with reality and life, and therefore fugitive and intangible. Science comprehends the thought of the reality, not reality itself; the thought of life, not life. That is its limit, its only really insuperable limit, because it is founded on the very nature of thought, which is the only organ of science.

Upon this nature are based the indisputable rights and grand mission of science, but also its vital impotence and even its mischievous action whenever, through its official licensed representatives, it arrogantly claims the right to govern life. The mission of science is, by observation of the general relations of passing and real facts, to establish the general laws inherent in the development of the phenomena of the physical and social world; it fixes, so to speak, the unchangeable landmarks of humanity's progressive march by indicating the general conditions which it is necessary to rigorously observe and always fatal to ignore or forget. In a word, science is the compass of life; but it is not life. Science is unchangeable, impersonal, general, abstract, insensible, like the laws of which it is but the ideal reproduction, reflected or mental—that is cerebral (using this word to remind us that science itself is but a material product of a material organ, the brain). Life is wholly fugitive and temporary, but also wholly palpitating with reality and individuality, sensibility, sufferings, joys, aspirations, needs, and passions. It alone spontaneously creates real things and beings. Science creates nothing; it establishes and recognises only the creations of life. And every time that scientific men, emerging from their abstract world, mingle with living creation in the real world, all that they propose or create is poor, ridiculously abstract, bloodless and lifeless, still-born, like the homunculus created by Wagner, the pedantic disciple of the immortal Doctor Faust. It follows that the only mission of science is to enlighten life, not to govern it.

The government of science and of men of science, even be they positivists, disciples of Auguste Comte, or, again, disciples of the doctrinaire; school of German Communism, cannot fail to be impotent, ridiculous, inhuman, cruel, oppressive, exploiting, maleficent. We may say of men of science, as such, what I have said of theologians and metaphysicians: they have neither sense nor heart for individual and living beings. We cannot even blame them for this, for it is the natural consequence of their profession. In so far as they are men of science, they have to deal with and can take interest in nothing except generalities; that do the laws. . . they are not exclusively men of science, but are also more or less men of life.

III.

Nevertheless, we must not rely too much on this. Though we may be well nigh certain that a savant would not dare to treat a man today as he treats a rabbit, it remains always to be feared that the savants, as a body, if not interfered with, may submit living men to scientific experiments, undoubtedly less cruel but none the less disagreeable to their victims. If they cannot perform experiments upon the bodies of individuals, they will ask nothing better than to perform them on the social body, and that what must be absolutely prevented.

In their existing organisation, monopolising science and remaining thus outside of social life, the savants form a separate caste, in many respects analogous to the priesthood. Scientific abstractions is their God, living and real individuals are their victims, and they are the consecrated and licensed sacrificers.

Science cannot go outside of the sphere of abstractions. In this respect it is infinitely inferior to art, which, in its turn, is peculiarly concerned also with general types and general situations, but which incarnates them by an artifice of its own in forms which, if they are not living in the sense of real life, none the less excite in our imagination the memory and sentiment of life; art in a certain sense individualizes the types and situations which it conceives by means of the individualities without flesh and bone, and consequently permanent and immortal, which it has the power to create; it recalls to our minds the living, real individualities which appear and disappear under our eyes. Art, then, is as it were the return of abstraction to life; science, on the contrary, is the perpetual immolation of life, fugitive, temporary, but real, on the altar of eternal abstractions.

Science is as incapable of grasping the individuality of a man as that of a rabbit, being equally indifferent to both. Not that it is ignorant of the principle of individuality: it conceives it perfectly as a principle, but not as a fact. It knows very well that all the animal species, including the human species, have no real existence outside of an indefinite number of individuals, born and dying to make room for new individuals equally fugitive. It knows that in rising from the animal species to the superior species the principle of individuality becomes more pronounced; the individuals appear freer and more complete. It knows that man, the last and most perfect animal of earth, presents the most complete and most remarkable individuality, because of his power to conceive, concrete, personify, as it were, in his social and private existence, the universal law. It knows, finally, when it is not vitiated by theological or metaphysical, political or judicial doctrinairism, or even by a narrow scientific pride, when it is not deaf to the instincts and spontaneous aspirations of life—it knows (and this is its last word) that respect for man is the supreme law of Humanity, and that the great, the real object of history, its only legitimate object is the humanization and emancipation, the real liberty, the prosperity and happiness of each individual living in society. For, if we would not fall back into the liberticidal fiction of the public welfare represented by the State, a fiction always founded on the systematic sacrifice of the people, we must clearly recognize that collective liberty and prosperity exist only so far as they represent the sum of individual liberties and prosperities.

Science knows all these things, but it does not and cannot go beyond them. Abstraction being its very nature, it can well enough conceive the principle of real and living individuality, but it can have no dealings with real and living individuals; it concerns itself with individuals in general, but not with Peter or James, not with such or such a one, who, so far as it is concerned, do not, cannot, have any existence. Its individuals, I repeat, are only abstractions.

Now, history is made, not by abstract individuals, but by acting, living and passing individuals. Abstractions advance only when borne forward by real men. For these beings made, not in idea only, but in reality of flesh and blood, science has no heart: it considers them at most as material for intellectual and social development. What does it care for the particular conditions and chance fate of Peter or James? It would make itself ridiculous, it would abdicate, it would annihilate itself, if it wished to concern itself with them otherwise than as examples in support of its eternal theories. And it would be ridiculous to wish it to do so, for its mission lies not there. It cannot grasp the concrete; it can move only in abstractions. Its mission is to busy itself with the situation and the general conditions of the existence and development, either of the human species in general, or of such a race, such a people, such a class or category of individuals; the general causes of their prosperity, their decline, and the best general methods of securing, their progress in all ways. Provided it accomplishes this task broadly and rationally, it will do its whole duty, and it would be really unjust to expect more of it.

But it would be equally ridiculous, it would be disastrous, to entrust it with a mission which it is incapable of fulfilling. Since its own nature forces it to ignore the existence of Peter and James, it must never be permitted, nor must anybody be permitted in its name, to govern Peter and James. For it were capable of treating them almost as it treats rabbits. Or rather, it would continue to ignore them; but its licensed representatives, men not at all abstract, but on the contrary in very active life and having very substantial interests, yielding to the pernicious influence which privilege inevitably exercises upon men, would finally fleece other men in the name of science, just as they have been fleeced hitherto by priests, politicians of all shades, and lawyers, in the name of God, of the State, of judicial Right.

What I preach then is, to a certain extent, the revolt of life against science, or rather against the government of science, not to destroy science—that would be high treason to humanity—but to remand it to its place so that it can never leave it again. Until now all human history has been only a perpetual and bloody immolation of millions of poor human beings in honor of some pitiless abstraction—God, country, power of State, national honor, historical rights, judicial rights, political liberty, public welfare. Such has been up to today the natural, spontaneous, and inevitable movement of human societies. We cannot undo it; we must submit to it so far as the past is concerned, as we submit to all natural fatalities. We must believe that that was the only possible way, to educate the human race. For we must not deceive ourselves: even in attributing the larger part to the Machiavellian wiles of the governing classes, we have to recognize that no minority would have been powerful enough to impose all these horrible sacrifices upon the masses if there had not been in the masses themselves a dizzy spontaneous movement which pushed them on to continual self-sacrifice, now to one, now to another of these devouring abstractions, the vampires of history ever nourished upon human blood.

We readily understand that this is very gratifying to the theologians, politicians, and jurists. Priests of these abstractions, they live only by the continual immolation of the people. Nor is it more surprising that metaphysics, too, should give its consent. Its only mission is to justify and rationalize as far as possible the iniquitous and absurd. But that positive science itself should have shown the same tendencies is a fact which we must deplore while we establish it. That it has done so is due to two reasons: in the first place, because, constituted outside of life, it is represented by a privileged body; and in the second place, because thus far it has posited itself as an absolute and final object of all human development. By a judicious criticism, which it can and finally will be forced to pass upon itself, it would understand, on the contrary, that it is only a means for the realization of a much higher object—that of the complete humanization of the real situation of all the real individuals who are born, who live, and who die, on earth.

The immense advantage of positive science over theology, metaphysics, politics, and judicial right consists in this—that, in place of the false and fatal abstractions set up by these doctrines, it posits true abstractions which express the general nature and logic of things, their general relations, and the general laws of their development. This separates it profoundly from all preceding doctrines, and will assure it forever a great position in society: it will constitute in a certain sense society's collective consciousness. But there is one aspect in which it resembles all these doctrines: its only possible object being abstractions, it is forced by its very nature to ignore real men, outside of whom the truest abstractions have no existence. To remedy this radical defect, positive science will have to proceed by a different method from that followed by the doctrines of the past. The latter have taken advantage of the ignorance of the masses to sacrifice them with delight to their abstractions, which by the way are always very lucrative to those who represent them in flesh and bone. Positive science, recognizing its absolute inability to conceive real individuals and interest itself in their lot, must definitely and absolutely renounce all claim to the government of societies; for if it should meddle therein, it would only sacrifice continually the living men whom it ignores to the abstractions which constitute the sole object of its legitimate preoccupations.

The true science of history, for instance, does not yet exist; scarcely do we begin today to catch a glimpse of its extremely complicated conditions. But suppose it were definitely developed, what could it give us? It would exhibit a faithful and rational picture of the natural development of the general conditions—material and ideal, economical, political and social, religious, philosophical, aesthetic, and scientific—of the societies which have a history. But this universal picture of human civilization, however detailed it might be, would never show anything beyond general and consequently abstract estimates. The milliards of individuals who have furnished the living and suffering materials of this history at once triumphant and dismal—triumphant by its general results, dismal by the immense hecatomb of human victims "crushed under its car"—those milliards of obscure individuals without whom none of the great abstract results of history would have been obtained—and who, bear in mind, have never benefited by any of these results—will find no place, not even the slightest in our annals. They have lived and been sacrificed, crushed for the good of abstract humanity, that is all.

Shall we blame the science of history? That would be unjust and ridiculous. Individuals cannot be grasped by thought, by reflection, or even by human speech, which is capable of expressing abstractions only; they cannot be grasped in the present day any more than in the past. Therefore social science itself, the science of the future, will necessarily continue to ignore them. All that we have a right to demand of it is that it shall point us with faithful and sure hand to the general causes of individual suffering—among these causes it will not forget the immolation and subordination (still too frequent, alas!) of living individuals to abstract generalities—at the same time showing us the general conditions necessary to the real emancipation of the individuals living in society. That is its mission; those are its limits, beyond which the action of social science can be only impotent and fatal. Beyond those limits being the doctrinaire and governmental pretentious of its licensed representatives, its priests. It is time to have done with all popes and priests; we want them no longer, even if they call themselves Social Democrats.

Once more, the sole mission of science is to light the road. Only Life, delivered from all its governmental and doctrinaire barriers, and given full liberty of action, can create.

How solve this antinomy?

On the one hand, science is indispensable to the rational organization of society; on the other, being incapable of interesting itself in that which is real and living, it must not interfere with the real or practical organization of society.

This contradiction can be solved only in one way: by the liquidation of science as a moral being existing outside the life of all, and represented by a body of breveted savants; it must spread among the masses. Science, being called upon to henceforth represent society's collective consciousness, must really become the property of everybody. Thereby, without losing anything of its universal character, of which it can never divest itself without ceasing to be science, and while continuing to concern itself exclusively with general causes, the conditions and fixed relations of individuals and things, it will become one in fact with the immediate and real life of all individuals. That will be a movement analogous to that which said to the Protestants at the beginning of the Reformation that there was no further need of priests for man, who would henceforth be his own priest; every man, thanks to the invisible intervention of the Lord Jesus Christ alone, having at last succeeded in swallowing his good God. But here the question is not of Jesus Christ, nor good God, nor of political liberty, nor of judicial right—things all theologically or metaphysically revealed, and all alike indigestible. The world of scientific abstractions is not revealed; it is inherent in the real world, of which it is only the general or abstract expression and representation. As long as it forms a separate region, specially represented by the savants as a body, this ideal world threatens to take the place of a good God to the real world, reserving for its licensed representatives the office of priests. That is the reason why it is necessary to dissolve the special social organization of the savants by general instruction, equal for all in all things, in order that the masses, ceasing to be flocks led and shorn by privileged priests, may take into their own hands the direction of their destinies.

But until the masses shall have reached this degree of instruction, will it be necessary to leave them to the government of scientific men? Certainly not. It would be better for them to dispense with science than allow themselves to be governed by savants. The first consequence of the government of these men would be to render science inaccessible to the people, and such a government would necessarily be aristocratic because the existing scientific institutions are essentially aristocratic. An aristocracy of learning! From the practical point of view the most implacable, and from the social point of view the most haughty and insulting—such would be the power established in the name of science. This régime would be capable of paralyzing the life and movement of society. The savants, always presumptuous, ever self-sufficient and ever impotent, would desire to meddle with everything, and the sources of life would dry up under the breath of their abstractions.

Once more, Life, not science, creates life; the spontaneous action of the people themselves alone can create liberty. Undoubtedly it would be a very fortunate thing if science could, from this day forth, illuminate the spontaneous march of the people towards their emancipation. But better an absence of light than a false and feeble light, kindled only to mislead those who follow it. After all, the people will not lack light. Not in vain have they traversed a long historic career, and paid for their errors by centuries of misery. The practical summary of their painful experiences constitutes a sort of traditional science, which in certain respects is worth as much as theoretical science. Last of all, a portion of the youth—those of the bourgeois students who feel hatred enough for the falsehood, hypocrisy, injustice, and cowardice of the bourgeoisie to find courage to turn their backs upon it, and passion enough to unreservedly embrace the just and human cause of the proletariat—those will be, as I have already said, fraternal instructors of the people; thanks to them, there will be no occasion for the government of the savants.

If the people should beware of the government of the savants, all the more should they provide against that of the inspired idealists. The more sincere these believers and poets of heaven, the more dangerous they become. The scientific abstraction, I have said, is a rational abstraction, true in its essence, necessary to life, of which it is the theoretical representation, or, if one prefers, the conscience. It may, it must, be absorbed and digested by life. The idealistic abstraction, God, is a corrosive poison, which destroys and decomposes life, falsifies and kills it. The pride of the idealists, not being personal but divine, is invincible and inexorable: it may, it must, die, but it will never yield, and while it has a breath left it will try to subject men to its God, just as the lieutenants of Prussia, these practical idealists of Germany, would like to see the people crushed under the spurred boot of their emperor. The faith is the same, the end but little different, and the result, as that of faith, is slavery.

It is at the same time the triumph of the ugliest and most brutal materialism. There is no need to demonstrate this in the case of Germany; one would have to be blind to avoid seeing it at the present hour. But I think it is still necessary to demonstrate it in the case of divine idealism.

Man, like all the rest of nature, is an entirely material being. The mind, the facility of thinking, of receiving and reflecting upon different external and internal sensations, of remembering them when they have passed and reproducing them by the imagination, of comparing and distinguishing them, of abstracting determinations common to them and thus creating general concepts, and finally of forming ideas by grouping and combining concepts according to different methods— intelligence, in a word, sole creator of our whole, ideal world, is a property of the animal body and especially of the quite material organism of the brain.

We know this certainly, by the experience of all, which no fact has ever contradicted and which any man can verify at any moment of his life. In all animals, without excepting the wholly inferior species, we find a certain degree of intelligence, and we see that, in the series of species, animal intelligence develops in proportion as the organization of a species approaches that of man, but that in man alone it attains to that power of abstraction which properly constitutes thought.

Universal experience, which is the sole origin, the source of all our knowledge, shows us, therefore, that all intelligence is always attached to some animal body, and that the intensity, the power, of this animal function depends on the relative perfection of the organism. The latter of these results of universal experience is not applicable only to the different animal species; we establish it likewise in men, whose intellectual and moral power depends so clearly upon the greater or less perfection of their organism as a race, as a nation, as a class, and as individuals, that it is not necessary to insist upon this point.

On the other hand, it is certain that no man has ever seen or can see pure mind, detached from all material form, existing separately from any animal body whatsoever. But if no person has seen it, how is it that men have come to believe in its existence? The fact of this belief is certain and if not universal, as all the idealists pretend, at least very general, and as such it is entirely worthy of our closest attention, for a general belief, however foolish it may be, exercises too potent a sway over the destiny of men to warrant us in ignoring it or putting it aside.

The explanation of this belief, moreover, is rational enough. The example afforded us by children and young people, and even by many men long past the age of majority, shows us that man may use his mental faculties for a long time before accounting to himself for the way in which he uses them, before becoming clearly conscious of it. During this working of the mind unconscious of itself, during this action of innocent or believing intelligence, man, obsessed by the external world, pushed on by that internal goad called life and its manifold necessities, creates a quantity of imaginations, concepts, and ideas necessarily very imperfect at first and conforming but slightly to the reality of the things and facts which they endeavour to express Not having yet the consciousness of his own intelligent action, not knowing yet that he himself has produced and continues to produce these imaginations, these concepts, these ideas, ignoring their wholly subjective — that is, human origin, he must naturally consider them as objective beings, as real beings, wholly independent of him, existing by themselves and in themselves.

It was thus that primitive peoples, emerging slowly from their animal innocence, created their gods. Having created them, not suspecting that they themselves were the real creators, they worshipped them; considering them as real beings infinitely superior to themselves, they attributed omnipotence to them, and recognised themselves as their creatures, their slaves. As fast as human ideas develop, the gods, who, as I have already stated, were never anything more than a fantastic, ideal, poetical reverberation of an inverted image, become idealised also. At first gross fetishes, they gradually become pure spirits, existing outside of the visible world, and at last, in the course of a long historic evolution, are confounded in a single Divine Being, pure, eternal, absolute Spirit, creator and master of the worlds.

In every development, just or false, real or imaginary collective or individual, it is always the first step, the first act that is the most difficult. That step once taken, the rest follows naturally as a necessary consequence. The difficult step in the historical development of this terrible religious insanity which continues to obsess and crush us was to posit a divine world as such, outside the world. This first act of madness, so natural from the physiological point of view and consequently necessary in the history of humanity, was not accomplished at a single stroke. I know not how many centuries were needed to develop this belief and make it a governing influence upon the mental customs of men. But, once established, it became omnipotent, as each insane notion necessarily becomes when it takes possession of man's brain. Take a madman, whatever the object of his madness — you will find that obscure and fixed idea which obsesses him seems to him the most natural thing in the world, and that, on the contrary, the real things which contradict this idea seem to him ridiculous and odious follies. Well religion is a collective insanity, the more powerful because it is traditional folly, and because its origin is lost in the most remote antiquity. As collective insanity it has penetrated to the very depths of the public and private existence of the peoples; it is incarnate in society; it has become, so to speak, the collective soul and thought. Every man is enveloped in it from his birth; he sucks it in with his mother's milk, absorbs it with all that he touches, all that he sees. He is so exclusively fed upon it, so poisoned and penetrated by it in all his being that later, however powerful his natural mind, he has to make unheard-of efforts to deliver himself from it, and then never completely succeeds. We have one proof of this in our modern idealists, and another in our doctrinaire materialists — the German Communists. They have found no way to shake off the religion of the State.

The supernatural world, the divine world, once well established in the imagination of the peoples, the development of the various religious systems has followed its natural and logical course, conforming, moreover, in all things to the contemporary development of economical and political relations of which it has been in all ages, in the world of religious fancy, the faithful reproduction and divine consecration. Thus has the collective and historical insanity which calls itself religion been developed since fetishism, passing through all the stages from polytheism to Christian monotheism.

The second step in the development of religious beliefs, undoubtedly the most difficult next to the establishment of a separate divine world, was precisely this transition from polytheism to monotheism, from the religious materialism of the pagans to the spiritualistic faith of the Christians. The pagan gods—and this was their principal characteristic—were first of all exclusively national gods. Very numerous, they necessarily retained a more or less material character, or, rather, they were so numerous because they were material, diversity being one of the principal attributes of the real world. The pagan gods were not yet strictly the negation of real things; they were only a fantastic exaggeration of them.

We have seen how much this transition cost the Jewish people, constituting, so to speak, its entire history. In vain did Moses and the prophets preach the one god; the people always relapsed into their primitive idolatry, into the ancient and comparatively much more natural and convenient faith in many good gods, more material, more human, and more palpable. Jehovah himself, their sole God, the God of Moses and the prophets, was still an extremely national God, who, to reward and punish his faithful followers, his chosen people, used material arguments, often stupid, always gross and cruel. It does not even appear that faith in his existence implied a negation of the existence of earlier gods. The Jewish God did not deny the existence of these rivals; he simply did not want his people to worship them side by side with him, because before all Jehovah was a very Jealous God. His first commandment was this:

"I am the Lord thy God, and thou shalt have no other gods before me."

Jehovah, then, was only a first draft, very material and very rough, of the supreme deity of modern idealism. Moreover, he was only a national God, like the Russian God worshipped by the German generals, subjects of the Czar and patriots of the empire of all the Russias; like the German God, whom the pietists and the German generals, subjects of William I at Berlin, will no doubt soon proclaim. The supreme being cannot be a national God; he must be the God of entire Humanity. Nor can the supreme being be a material being; he must be the negation of all matter — pure spirit. Two things have proved necessary to the realisation of the worship of the supreme being: (1) a realisation, such as it is, of Humanity by the negation of nationalities and national forms of worship; (2) a development, already far advanced, of metaphysical ideas in order to spiritualise the gross Jehovah of the Jews.

The first condition was fulfilled by the Romans, though in a very negative way no doubt, by the conquest of most of the countries known to the ancients and by the destruction of their national institutions. The gods of all the conquered nations, gathered in the Pantheon, mutually cancelled each other. This was the first draft of humanity, very gross and quite negative.

As for the second condition, the spiritualisation of Jehovah, that was realised by the Greeks long before the conquest of their country by the Romans. They were the creators of metaphysics. Greece, in the cradle of her history, had already found from the Orient a divine world which had been definitely established in the traditional faith of her peoples; this world had been left and handed over to her by the Orient. In her instinctive period, prior to her political history, she had developed and prodigiously humanised this divine world through her poets; and when she actually began her history, she already had a religion readymade, the most sympathetic and noble of all the religions which have existed, so far at least as a religion — that is, a lie — can be noble and sympathetic. Her great thinkers — and no nation has had greater than Greece — found the divine world established, not only outside of themselves in the people, but also in themselves as a habit of feeling and thought, and naturally they took it as a point of departure. That they made no theology — that is, that they did not wait in vain to reconcile dawning reason with the absurdities of such a god, as did the scholastics of the Middle Ages — was already much in their favour. They left the gods out of their speculations and attached themselves directly to the divine idea, one, invisible, omnipotent, eternal, and absolutely spiritualistic but impersonal. As concerns Spiritualism, then, the Greek metaphysicians, much more than the Jews, were the creators of the Christian god. The Jews only added to it the brutal personality of their Jehovah.

That a sublime genius like the divine Plato could have been absolutely convinced of the reality of the divine idea shows us how contagious, how omnipotent, is the tradition of the religious mania even on the greatest minds. Besides, we should not be surprised at it, since, even in our day, the greatest philosophical genius which has existed since Aristotle and Plato, Hegel—in spite even of Kant's criticism, imperfect and too metaphysical though it be, which had demolished the objectivity or reality of the divine ideas—tried to replace these divine ideas upon their transcendental or celestial throne. It is true that Hegel went about his work of restoration in so impolite a manner that he killed the good God forever. He took away from these ideas their divine halo, by showing to whoever will read him that they were never anything more than a creation of the human mind running through history in search of itself. To put an end to all religious insanities and the divine mirage, he left nothing lacking but the utterance of those grand words which were said after him, almost at the same time, by two great minds who had never heard of each other—Ludwig Feuerbach, the disciple and demolisher of Hegel, in Germany, and Auguste Comte, the founder of positive philosophy, in France. These words were as follows:

"Metaphysics are reduced to psychology." All the metaphysical systems have been nothing else than human psychology developing itself in history.

Today it is no longer difficult to understand how the divine ideas were born, how they were created in succession by the abstractive faculty of man. Man made the gods. But in the time of Plato this knowledge was impossible. The collective mind, and consequently the individual mind as well, even that of the greatest genius, was not ripe for that. Scarcely had it said with Socrates: "Know thyself!" This self-knowledge existed only in a state of intuition; in fact, it amounted to nothing. Hence it was impossible for the human mind to suspect that it was itself the sole creator of the divine world. It found the divine world before it; it found it as history, as tradition, as a sentiment, as a habit of thought; and it necessarily made it the object of its loftiest speculations. Thus was born metaphysics, and thus were developed and perfected the divine ideas, the basis of Spiritualism.

It is true that after Plato there was a sort of inverse movement in the development of the mind. Aristotle, the true father of science and positive philosophy, did not deny the divine world, but concerned himself with it as little as possible. He was the first to study, like the analyst and experimenter that he was, logic, the laws of human thought, and at the same time the physical world, not in its ideal, illusory essence, but in its real aspect. After him the Greeks of Alexandria established the first school of the positive scientists. They were atheists. But their atheism left no mark on their contemporaries. Science tended more and more to separate itself from life. After Plato, divine ideas were rejected in metaphysics themselves; this was done by the Epicureans and Sceptics, two sects who contributed much to the degradation of human aristocracy, but they had no effect upon the masses.

Another school, infinitely more influential, was formed at Alexandria. This was the school of neo-Platonists. These, confounding in an impure mixture the monstrous imaginations of the Orient with the ideas of Plato, were the true originators, and later the elaborators, of the Christian dogmas.

Thus the personal and gross egoism of Jehovah, the not less brutal and gross Roman conquest, and the metaphysical ideal speculation of the Greeks, materialised by contact with the Orient, were the three historical elements which made up the spiritualistic religion of the Christians.

Before the altar of a unique and supreme God was raised on the ruins of the numerous altars of the pagan gods, the autonomy of the various nations composing the pagan or ancient world had to be destroyed first. This was very brutally done by the Romans who, by conquering the greatest part of the globe known to the ancients, laid the first foundations, quite gross and negative ones no doubt, of humanity. A God thus raised above the national differences, material and social, of all countries, and in a certain sense the direct negation of them, must necessarily be an immaterial and abstract being. But faith in the existence of such a being, so difficult a matter, could not spring into existence suddenly. Consequently, as I have demonstrated in the Appendix, it went through a long course of preparation and development at the hands of Greek metaphysics, which were the first to establish in a philosophical manner the notion of the divine idea, a model eternally creative and always reproduced by the visible world. But the divinity conceived and created by Greek philosophy was an impersonal divinity. No logical and serious metaphysics being able to rise, or, rather, to descend, to the idea of a personal God, it became necessary, therefore, to imagine a God who was one and very personal at once. He was found in the very brutal, selfish, and cruel person of Jehovah, the national God of the Jews. But the Jews, in spite of that exclusive national spirit which distinguishes them even today, had become in fact, long before the birth of Christ, the most international people of the world. Some of them carried away as captives, but many more even urged on by that mercantile passion which constitutes one of the principal traits of their character, they had spread through all countries, carrying everywhere the worship of their Jehovah, to whom they remained all the more faithful the more he abandoned them.

In Alexandria this terrible god of the Jews made the personal acquaintance of the metaphysical divinity of Plato, already much corrupted by Oriental contact, and corrupted her still more by his own. In spite of his national, jealous, and ferocious exclusivism, he could not long resist the graces of this ideal and impersonal divinity of the Greeks. He married her, and from this marriage was born the spiritualistic — but not spirited — God of the Christians. The neoplatonists of Alexandria are known to have been the principal creators of the Christian theology.

Nevertheless theology alone does not make a religion, any more than historical elements suffice to create history. By historical elements I mean the general conditions of any real development whatsoever — for example in this case the conquest of the world by the Romans and the meeting of the God of the Jews with the ideal of divinity of the Greeks. To impregnate the historical elements, to cause them to run through a series of new historical transformations, a living, spontaneous fact was needed, without which they might have remained many centuries longer in the state of unproductive elements. This fact was not lacking in Christianity: it was the propagandism, martyrdom, and death of Jesus Christ.

We know almost nothing of this great and saintly personage, all that the gospels tell us being contradictory, and so fabulous that we can scarcely seize upon a few real and vital traits. But it is certain that he was the preacher of the poor, the friend and consoler of the wretched, of the ignorant, of the slaves, and of the women, and that by these last he was much loved. He promised eternal life to all who are oppressed, to all who suffer here below; and the number is immense. He was hanged, as a matter of course, by the representatives of the official morality and public order of that period. His disciples and the disciples of his disciples succeeded in spreading, thanks to the destruction of the national barriers by the Roman conquest, and propagated the Gospel in all the countries known to the ancients. Everywhere they were received with open arms by the slaves and the women, the two most oppressed, most suffering, and naturally also the most ignorant classes of the ancient world. For even such few proselytes as they made in the privileged and learned world they were indebted in great part to the influence of women. Their most extensive propagandism was directed almost exclusively among the people, unfortunate and degraded by slavery. This was the first awakening, the first intellectual revolt of the proletariat.

The great honour of Christianity, its incontestable merit, and the whole secret of its unprecedented and yet thoroughly legitimate triumph, lay in the fact that it appealed to that suffering and immense public to which the ancient world, a strict and cruel intellectual and political aristocracy, denied even the simplest rights of humanity. Otherwise it never could have spread. The doctrine taught by the apostles of Christ, wholly consoling as it may have seemed to the unfortunate, was too revolting, too absurd from the standpoint of human reason, ever to have been accepted by enlightened men According with what joy the apostle Paul speaks of the *scandale de la foi*, and of the triumph of that divine *folie*; rejected by the powerful and wise of the century, but all the more passionately accepted by the simple, the ignorant, and the weak-minded!

Indeed there must have been a very deep-seated dissatisfaction with life, a very intense thirst of heart, and an almost absolute poverty of thought, to secure the acceptance of the Christian absurdity, the most audacious and monstrous of all religious absurdities.

This was not only the negation of all the political, social, and religious institutions of antiquity: it was the absolute overturn of common sense, of all human reason. The living being, the real world, were considered thereafter as nothing; whereas the product of man's abstractive faculty, the last and supreme abstraction in which this faculty, far beyond existing things, even beyond the most general determinations of the living being, the ideas of space and time, having nothing left to advance beyond, rests in contemplation of his emptiness and absolute immobility.

That abstraction, that *caput mortuum*, absolutely void of all contents, the true nothing, God, is proclaimed the only real, eternal, all-powerful being. The real All is declared nothing and the absolute nothing the All. The shadow becomes the substance and the substance vanishes like a shadow.

All this was audacity and absurdity unspeakable, the true *scandale de la foi*, the triumph of credulous stupidity over the mind for the masses; and — for a few — the triumphant irony of a mind wearied, corrupted, disillusioned, and disgusted in honest and serious search for truth; it was that necessity of shaking off thought and becoming brutally stupid so frequently felt by surfeited minds:

Credo quod absurdum.

I believe in the absurd; I believe in it, precisely and mainly, because it is absurd. In the same way many distinguished and enlightened minds in our day believe in animal magnetism, spiritualism, tipping tables, and—why go so far?—believe still in Christianity, in idealism, in God.

The belief of the ancient proletariat, like that of the modern, was more robust and simple, less *haut goût*. The Christian propagandism appealed to its heart, not to its mind; to its eternal aspirations, its necessities, its sufferings, its slavery, not to its reason, which still slept and therefore could know nothing about logical contradictions and the evidence of the absurd. It was interested solely in knowing when the hour of promised deliverance would strike, when the kingdom of God would come. As for theological dogmas, it did not trouble itself about them because it understood nothing about them. The proletariat converted to Christianity constituted its growing material but not its intellectual strength.

As for the Christian dogmas, it is known that they were elaborated in a series of theological and literary works and in the Councils, principally by the converted neo-Platonists of the Orient. The Greek mind had fallen so low that, in the fourth century of the Christian era, the period of the first Council, the idea of a personal God, pure, eternal, absolute mind, creator and supreme master, existing outside of the world, was unanimously accepted by the Church Fathers; as a logical consequence of this absolute absurdity, it then became natural and necessary to believe in the immateriality and immortality of the human soul, lodged and imprisoned in a body only partially mortal, there being in this body itself a portion which, while material, is immortal like the soul, and must be resurrected with it. We see how difficult it was, even for the Church Fathers, to conceive pure minds outside of any material form. It should be added that, in general, it is the character of every metaphysical and theological argument to seek to explain one absurdity by another.

It was very fortunate for Christianity that it met a world of slaves. It had another piece of good luck in the invasion of the Barbarians. The latter were worthy people, full of natural force, and, above all, urged on by a great necessity of life and a great capacity for it; brigands who had stood every test, capable of devastating and gobbling up anything, like their successors, the Germans of today; but they were much less systematic and pedantic than these last, much less moralistic, less learned, and on the other hand much more independent and proud, capable of science and not incapable of liberty, as are the bourgeois of modern Germany. But, in spite of all their great qualities, they were nothing but barbarians — that is, as indifferent to all questions of theology and metaphysics as the ancient slaves, a great number of whom, moreover, belonged to their race. So that, their practical repugnance once overcome, it was not difficult to convert them theoretically to Christianity.

For ten centuries Christianity, armed with the omnipotence of Church and State and opposed by no competition, was able to deprave, debase, and falsify the mind of Europe. It had no competitors, because outside of the Church there were neither thinkers nor educated persons. It alone thought, it alone spoke and wrote, it alone taught. Though heresies arose in its bosom, they affected only the theological or practical developments of the fundamental dogma, never that dogma itself. The belief in God, pure spirit and creator of the world, and the belief in the immateriality of the soul remained untouched. This double belief became the ideal basis of the whole Occidental and Oriental civilization of Europe; it penetrated and became incarnate in all the institutions, all the details of the public and private life of all classes, and the masses as well.

After that, is it surprising that this belief has lived until the present day, continuing to exercise its disastrous influence even upon select minds, such as those of Mazzini, Michelet, Quinet, and so many others? We have seen that the first attack upon it came from the Renaissance; of the free mind in the fifteenth century, which produced heroes and martyrs like Vanini, Giordano Bruno, and Galileo. Although drowned in the noise, tumult, and passions of the Reformation, it noiselessly continued its invisible work, bequeathing to the noblest minds of each generation its task of human emancipation by the destruction of the absurd, until at last, in the latter half of the eighteenth century, it again reappeared in broad day, boldly waving the flag of atheism and materialism.

The human mind, then, one might have supposed, was at last about to deliver itself from all the divine obsessions. Not at all. The divine falsehood upon which humanity had been feeding for eighteen centuries (speaking of Christianity only) was once more to show itself more powerful than human truth. No longer able to make use of the black tribe, of the ravens consecrated by the Church, of the Catholic or Protestant priests, all confidence in whom had been lost, it made use of lay priests, short-robed liars and sophists, among whom the principal roles devolved upon two fatal men, one the falsest mind, the other the most doctrinally despotic will, of the last century—J. J. Rousseau and Robespierre.

The first is the perfect type of narrowness and suspicious meanness, of exaltation without other object than his own person, of cold enthusiasm and hypocrisy at once sentimental and implacable, of the falsehood of modern idealism. He may be considered as the real creator of modern reaction. To all appearance the most democratic writer of the eighteenth century, he bred within himself the pitiless despotism of the statesman. He was the prophet of the doctrinaire State, as Robespierre, his worthy and faithful disciple, tried to become its high priest. Having heard the saying of Voltaire that, if God did not exist, it would be necessary to invent him, J. J. Rousseau invented the Supreme Being, the abstract and sterile God of the deists. And it was in the name of the Supreme Being, and of the hypocritical virtue commanded by this Supreme Being, that

Robespierre guillotined first the Hébertists and then the very genius of the Revolution, Danton, in whose person he assassinated the Republic, thus preparing the way for the thenceforth necessary triumph of the dictatorship of Bonaparte I. After this great triumph, the idealistic reaction sought and found servants less fanatical, less terrible nearer to the diminished stature of the actual bourgeoisie. In France, Chateaubriand, Lamartine, and — shall I say it? Why not? All must be said if it is truth — Victor Hugo himself, the democrat, the republican, the quasi-socialist of today! And after them the whole melancholy and sentimental company of poor and pallid minds who, under the leadership of these masters, established the modern romantic school in Germany, the Schlegels, the Tiecks, the Novalis, the Werners, the Schellings, and so many others besides, whose names do not even deserve to be recalled.

The literature created by this school was the very reign of ghosts and phantoms. It could not stand the sunlight; the twilight alone permitted it to live. No more could it stand the brutal contact of the masses. It was the literature of the tender, delicate, distinguished souls, aspiring to heaven, and living on earth as if in spite of themselves. It had a horror and contempt for the politics and questions of the day; but when perchance it referred to them, it showed itself frankly reactionary, took the side of the Church against the insolence of the freethinkers, of the kings against the peoples, and of all the aristocrats against the vile rabble of the streets. For the rest, as I have just said, the dominant feature of the school of romanticism was a quasi-complete indifference to politics. Amid the clouds in which it lived could be distinguished two real points — the rapid development of bourgeois materialism and the ungovernable outburst of individual vanities.

To understand this romantic literature, the reason for its existence must be sought in the transformation which had been effected in the bosom of the bourgeois class since the revolution of 1793.

From the Renaissance and the Reformation down to the Revolution, the bourgeoisie, if not in Germany, at least in Italy, in France, in Switzerland, in England, in Holland, was the hero and representative of the revolutionary genius of history. From its bosom sprang most of the freethinkers of the fifteenth century, the religious reformers of the two following centuries, and the apostles of human emancipation, including this time those of Germany, of the past century. It alone, naturally supported by the powerful arm of the people, who had faith in it, made the revolution of 1789 and '93. It proclaimed the downfall of royalty and of the Church, the fraternity of the peoples, the rights of man and of the citizen. Those are its titles to glory; they are immortal!

Soon it split. A considerable portion of the purchasers of national property having become rich, and supporting themselves no longer on the proletariat of the cities, but on the major portion of the peasants of France, these also having become landed proprietors, had no aspiration left but for peace, the re-establishment of public order, and the foundation of a strong and regular government. It therefore welcomed with joy the dictatorship of the first Bonaparte, and, although always Voltairean, did not view with displeasure the Concordat with the Pope and the re-establishment of the official Church in France: "Religion is so necessary to the people!" Which means that, satiated themselves, this portion of the bourgeoisie then began to see that it was needful to the maintenance of their situation and the preservation of their newly-acquired estates to appease the unsatisfied hunger of the people by promises of heavenly manna. Then it was that Chateaubriand began to preach.

Napoleon fell and the Restoration brought back into France the legitimate monarchy, and with it the power of the Church and of the nobles, who regained, if not the whole, at least a considerable portion of their former influence. This reaction threw the bourgeoisie back into the Revolution, and with the revolutionary spirit that of scepticism also was re-awakened in it. It set Chateaubriand aside and began to read Voltaire again; but it did not go so far as Diderot: its debilitated nerves could not stand nourishment so strong. Voltaire, on the contrary, at once a freethinker and a deist, suited it very well. Béranger and P. L. Courier expressed this new tendency perfectly. The God of the good people, and the ideal of the bourgeois king, at once liberal and democratic, sketched against the majestic and thenceforth inoffensive background of the Empire's gigantic victories, such was at that period the daily intellectual food of the bourgeoisie of France.

Lamartine, to be sure, excited by a vain and ridiculously envious desire to rise to the poetic height of the great Byron, had begun his coldly delirious hymns in honour of the God of the nobles and of the legitimate monarchy. But his songs resounded only in aristocratic salons. The bourgeoisie did not hear them. Béranger was its poet and Courier was its political writer.

The revolution of July resulted in lifting its tastes. We know that every bourgeois in France carries within him the imperishable type of the bourgeois gentleman, a type which never fails to appear immediately the *parvenu* acquires a little wealth and power. In 1830 the wealthy bourgeoisie had definitely replaced the old nobility in the seats of power. It naturally tended to establish a new aristocracy. An aristocracy of capital first of all, but also an aristocracy of intellect, of good manners and delicate sentiments. It began to feel religious.

This was not on its part simply an aping of aristocratic customs. It was also a necessity of its position. The proletariat had rendered it a final service in once more aiding it to overthrow the nobility. The bourgeoisie now had no further need of its co-operation, for it felt itself firmly seated in the shadow of the throne of July, and the alliance with the people, thenceforth useless, began to become inconvenient. It was necessary to remand it to its place, which naturally could not be done without provoking great indignation among the masses. It became necessary to restrain this indignation. In the name of what? In the name of the bourgeois interest bluntly confessed? That would have been much too cynical. The more unjust and inhuman an interest is, the greater need it has of sanction. Now, where find it if not in religion, that good protectress of all the well-fed and the useful consoler of the hungry? And more than ever the triumphant bourgeoisie saw that religion was indispensable to the people.

After having won all its titles to glory in religious, philosophical, and political opposition, in protest and in revolution, it at last became the dominant class and thereby even the defender and preserver of the State, thenceforth the regular institution of the exclusive power of that class. The State is force, and for it, first of all, is the right of force, the triumphant argument of the needle-gun, of the chassepot. But man is so singularly constituted that this argument, wholly eloquent as it may appear, is not sufficient in the long run. Some moral sanction or other is absolutely necessary to enforce his respect. Further, this sanction must be at once so simple and so plain that it may convince the masses, who, after having been reduced by the power of the State, must also be induced to morally recognise its right.

There are only two ways of convincing the masses of the goodness of any social institution whatever. The first, the only real one, but also the most difficult to adopt—because it implies the abolition of the State, or, in other words, the abolition of the organised political exploitation of the majority by any minority whatsoever—would be the direct and complete satisfaction of the needs and aspirations of the people, which would be equivalent to the complete liquidation of the political and economical existence of the bourgeois class, or, again, to the abolition of the State. Beneficial means for the masses, but detrimental to bourgeois interests; hence it is useless to talk about them.

The only way, on the contrary, harmful only to the people, precious in its salvation of bourgeois privileges, is no other than religion. That is the eternal mirage; which leads away the masses in a search for divine treasures, while much more reserved, the governing class contents itself with dividing among all its members—very unequally, moreover, and always giving most to him who possesses most—the miserable goods of earth and the plunder taken from the people, including their political and social liberty.

There is not, there cannot be, a State without religion. Take the freest States in the world—the United States of America or the Swiss Confederation, for instance—and see what an important part is played in all official discourses by divine Providence, that supreme sanction of all States.

But whenever a chief of State speaks of God, be he William I, the Knouto-Germanic emperor, or Grant, the president of the great republic, be sure that he is getting ready to shear once more his people-flock.

The French liberal and Voltairean bourgeoisie, driven by temperament to a positivism (not to say a materialism) singularly narrow and brutal, having become the governing class of the State by its triumph of 1830, had to give itself an official religion. It was not an easy thing. The bourgeoisie could not abruptly go back under the yoke of Roman Catholicism. Between it and the Church of Rome was an abyss of blood and hatred, and, however practical and wise one becomes, it is never possible to repress a passion developed by history. Moreover, the French bourgeoisie would have covered itself with ridicule if it had gone back to the Church to take part in the pious ceremonies of its worship, an essential condition of a meritorious and sincere conversion. Several attempted it, it is true, but their heroism was rewarded by no other result than a fruitless scandal. Finally, a return to Catholicism was impossible on account of the insolvable contradiction which separates the invariable politics of Rome from the development of the economical and political interests of the middle class.

In this respect Protestantism is much more advantageous. It is the bourgeois religion par excellence. It accords just as much liberty as is necessary to the bourgeois, and finds a way of reconciling celestial aspirations with the respect which terrestrial conditions demand. Consequently it is especially in Protestant countries that commerce and industry have been developed. But it was impossible for the French bourgeoisie to become Protestant. To pass from one religion to another—unless it be done deliberately, as sometimes in the case of the Jews of Russia and Poland, who get baptised three or four times in order to receive each time the remuneration allowed them—to seriously change one's religion, a little faith is necessary. Now, in the exclusive positive heart of the French bourgeois there is no room for faith. He professes the most profound indifference for all questions which touch neither his pocket first nor his social vanity afterwards. He is as indifferent to Protestantism as to Catholicism. On the other hand, the French bourgeois could not go over to Protestantism without putting himself in conflict with the Catholic routine of the majority of the French people, which would have been great imprudence on the part of a class pretending to govern the nation.

There was still one way left—to return to the humanitarian and revolutionary religion of the eighteenth century. But that would have led too far. So the bourgeoisie was obliged, in order to sanction its new State, to create a new religion which might be boldly proclaimed, without too much ridicule and scandal, by the whole bourgeois class.

Thus was born doctrinaire Deism.

Others have told, much better than I could tell it, the story of the birth and development of this school, which had so decisive and—we may well add—so fatal an influence on the political, intellectual, and moral education of the bourgeois youth of France. It dates from Benjamin Constant and Madame de Staël; its real founder was Royer-Collard; its apostles, Guizot, Cousin, Villemain, and many others. Its boldly avowed object was the reconciliation of Revolution with Reaction, or, to use the language of the school, of the principle of liberty with that of authority, and naturally to the advantage of the latter.

This reconciliation signified: in politics, the taking away of popular liberty for the benefit of bourgeois rule, represented by the monarchical and constitutional State; in philosophy, the deliberate submission of free reason to the eternal principles of faith. We have only to deal here with the latter.

We know that this philosophy was specially elaborated by M. Cousin, the father of French eclecticism. A superficial and pedantic talker, incapable of any original conception, of any idea peculiar to himself, but very strong on commonplace, which he confounded with common sense, this illustrious philosopher learnedly prepared, for the use of the studious youth of France, a metaphysical dish of his own making, the use of which, made compulsory in all schools of the State under the University, condemned several generations one after the other to a cerebral indigestion. Imagine a philosophical vinegar sauce of the most opposed systems, a mixture of Fathers of the Church, scholastic philosophers, Descartes and Pascal, Kant and Scotch psychologists, all this a superstructure on the divine and innate ideas of Plato, and covered up with a layer of Hegelian immanence, accompanied, of course, by an ignorance, as contemptuous as it is complete, of natural science, and proving just as two times two make five, the existence of a personal God.

Marxism, Freedom And The State

Chapter I; Introductory

I am a passionate seeker after Truth and a not less passionate enemy of the malignant fictions used by the "Party of Order", the official representatives of all turpitudes, religious, metaphysical, political, judicial, economic, and social, present and past, to brutalise and enslave the world; I am a fanatical lover of Liberty; considering it as the only medium in which can develop intelligence, dignity, and the happiness of man; not official "Liberty", licensed, measured and regulated by the State, a falsehood representing the privileges of a few resting on the slavery of everybody else; not the individual liberty, selfish, mean, and fictitious advanced by the school of Rousseau and all other schools of bourgeois Liberalism, which considers the rights of the individual as limited by the rights of the State, and therefore necessarily results in the reduction of the rights of the individual to zero.

No, I mean the only liberty which is truly worthy of the name, the liberty which consists in the full development of all the material, intellectual and moral powers which are to be found as faculties latent in everybody, the liberty which recognises no other restrictions than those which are traced for us by the laws of our own nature; so that properly speaking there are no restrictions, since these laws are not imposed on us by some outside legislator, beside us or above us; they are immanent in us, inherent, constituting the very basis of our being, material as well as intellectual and moral; instead, therefore, of finding them a limit, we must consider them as the real conditions and effective reason for our liberty.

I mean that liberty of each individual which, far from halting as at a boundary before the liberty of others, finds there its confirmation and its extension to infinity; the illimitable liberty of each through the liberty of all, liberty by solidarity, liberty in equality; liberty triumphing over brute force and the principle of authority which was never anything but the idealised expression of that force, liberty which, after having overthrown all heavenly and earthly idols, will found and organise a new world, that of human solidarity, on the ruins of all Churches and all States.

I am a convinced upholder of economic and social equality, because I know that, without that equality, liberty, justice, human dignity, morality, and the well-being of individuals as well as the prosperity of nations will never be anything else than so many lies. But as upholder in all circumstances of liberty, that first condition of humanity, I think that liberty must establish itself in the world by the spontaneous organisation of labour and of collective ownership by productive associations freely organised and federalised in districts, and by the equally spontaneous federation of districts, but not by the supreme and tutelary action of the State.

There is the point which principally divides the Revolutionary Socialists or Collectivists from the Authoritarian Communists, who are upholders of the absolute initiative of the State. Their goal is the same; each party desires equally the creation of a new social order founded only on the organisation of collective labour, inevitably imposed on each and every one by the very force of things, equal economic conditions for all, and the collective appropriation of the instruments of labour. Only the Communists imagine that they will be able to get there by the development and organisation of the political power of the working-classes, and principally of the proletariat of the towns, by the help of the bourgeois Radicalism, whilst the Revolutionary Socialists, enemies of all equivocal combinations and alliances, think on the contrary that they cannot reach this goal except by the development and organisation, not of the political but of the social and consequently anti-political power of the working masses of town and country alike, including all favourably disposed persons of the upper classes, who, breaking completely with their past, would be willing to join them and fully accept their programme.

Hence, two different methods. The Communists believe they must organise the workers' forces to take possession of the political power of the State. The Revolutionary Socialists organise with a view to the destruction, or if you prefer a politer word, the liquidation of the State. The Communists are the upholders of the principle and practice of authority, the Revolutionary Socialists have confidence only in liberty. Both equally supporters of that science which must kill superstition and replace faith, the former would wish to impose it; the latter will exert themselves to propagate it so that groups of human beings, convinced, will organise themselves and will federate spontaneously, freely, from below upwards, by their own movement and conformably to their real interests, but never after a plan traced in advance and imposed on the "ignorant masses" by some superior intellects.

The Revolutionary Socialists think that there is much more practical sense and spirit in the instinctive aspirations and in the real needs of the masses of the people than in the profound intellect of all these learned men and tutors of humanity who, after so many efforts have failed to make it happy, still presume to add their efforts. The Revolutionary Socialists think, on the contrary, that the human race has let itself long enough, too long, be governed, and that the source of its misfortunes does not lie in such or such form of government but in the very principle and fact of government, of whatever type it may be. It is, in fine, the contradiction already become historic, which exists between the Communism scientifically developed by the German school and accepted in part by the American and English Socialists on the one hand, and the Proudhonism largely developed and pushed to its last consequences, on the other hand, which is accepted by the proletariat of the Latin countries.

It has equally been accepted and will continue to be still more accepted by the essentially anti-political sentiment of the Slav peoples.

Chapter II; Marxist Ideology

The doctrinaire school of Socialists, or rather of German Authoritarian Communists, was founded a little before 1848, and has rendered, it must be recognised, eminent services to the cause of the proletariat not only in Germany, but in Europe. It is to them that belongs principally the great idea of an "International Workingmen's Association" and also the initiative for its first realisation. Today, they are to be found at the head of the Social Democratic Labour Party in Germany, having as its organ the "*Volksstaat*" ("The People's State").

It is therefore a perfectly respectable school which does not prevent it from displaying a very bad disposition sometimes, and above all from taking for the bases of its theories a principle which is profoundly true when one considers it in its true light, that is to say, from the relative point of view, but which when envisaged and set down in an absolute manner as the only foundation and first source of all other principles, as is done by this school, becomes completely false.

This principle, which constitutes besides the essential basis of scientific Socialism, was for the first time scientifically formulated and developed by Karl Marx, the principal leader of the German Communist school. It forms the dominating thought of the celebrated *Communist Manifesto* which an international Committee of French, English, Belgian and German Communists assembled in London issued in 1848 under the slogan: "Proletarians of all lands, unite" This manifesto, drafted as everyone knows, by Messrs. Marx and Engels, became the basis of all the further scientific works of the school and of the popular agitation later started by Ferdinand Lassalle in Germany.

This principle is the absolute opposite to that recognised by the Idealists of all schools. Whilst these latter derive all historical facts, including the development of material interests and of the different phases of the economic organisation of society, from the development of Ideas, the German Communists, on the contrary, want to see in all human history, in the most idealistic manifestations of the collective as well as the individual life of humanity, in all the intellectual, moral, religious, metaphysical, scientific, artistic, political, juridical, and social developments which have been produced in the past and continue to be produced in the present, nothing but the reflections or the necessary after-effects of the development of economic facts. Whilst the Idealists maintain that ideas dominate and produce facts, the Communists, in agreement besides with scientific Materialism say, on the contrary, that facts give birth to ideas and that these latter are never anything else but the ideal expression of accomplished facts and that among all the facts, economic and material facts, the pre-eminent facts, constitute the essential basis, the principal foundation of which all the other facts, intellectual and moral, political and social, are nothing more than the inevitable derivatives.

We, who are Materialists and Determinists just as much as Marx himself, we also recognise the inevitable linking of economic and political facts in history. We recognise, indeed, the necessity, the inevitable character of all events that happen, but we do not bow before them indifferently, and above all we are very careful about praising them when, by their nature, they show themselves in flagrant opposition to the supreme end of history, to the thoroughly human ideal that is to be found under more or less obvious forms, in the instincts, the aspirations of the people and under all the religious symbols of all epochs, because it is inherent in the human race, the most social of all the races of animals on earth. Thus this ideal, today better understood than ever, can be summed up in the words: It is the triumph of humanity, it is the conquest and accomplishment of the full freedom and full development, material, intellectual and moral, of every individual, by the absolutely free and spontaneous organisation of economic and social solidarity as completely as possible between all human beings living on the earth.

Everything in history that shows itself conformable to that end, from the human point of view — and we can have no other — is good; all that is contrary to it is bad. We know very well, in any case, that what we call good and bad are always, one and the other, the natural results of natural causes, and that consequently one is as inevitable as the other. But as in what is properly called Nature we recognise many necessities that we are little disposed to bless, for example the necessity of dying of hydrophobia when bitten by a mad dog, in the same way, in that immediate continuation of the life of Nature, called History, we encounter many necessities which we find much more worthy of opprobrium than of benediction and which we believe we should stigmatise with all the energy of which we are capable, in the interest of our social and individual morality, although we recognise that from the moment they have been accomplished, even the most detestable historic facts have that character of inevitability which is found in all the Phenomena of Nature as well as those of history.

To make my idea clearer, I shall illustrate it by some examples. When I study the respective social and political conditions in which the Romans and the Greeks came into contact towards the decline of Antiquity, I arrive at the conclusion that the conquest and destruction by the military and civic barbarism of the Romans of the comparatively high standard of human liberty of Greece was a logical, natural, absolutely inevitable fact. But that does not prevent me at all from taking retrospectively, and very firmly, the side of Greece against Rome in that struggle, and I find that the human race gained absolutely nothing by the triumph of the Romans.

In the same way, I consider as perfectly natural, logical, and consequently inevitable fact, that Christians should have destroyed with a holy fury all the libraries of the Pagans, all the treasures of Art, and of ancient philosophy and science. But it is absolutely impossible for me to grasp what advantages have resulted from it for our political and social development. I am even very much disposed to think that—apart from that inevitable process of economic facts in which, if one were to believe Marx, there must be sought to the exclusion of all other considerations the only cause of all the intellectual and moral facts which are produced in history—I say I am strongly disposed to think that this act of holy barbarity, or rather that long series of barbarous acts and crimes which the first Christians, divinely inspired, committed against the human spirit, was one of the principal causes of the intellectual and moral degradation and consequently also of the political and social enslavement which filled that long series of baneful centuries called the Middle Ages. Be sure of this, that if the first Christians had not destroyed the Libraries, Museums, and Temples of antiquity, we should not have been condemned today to fight the mass of horrible and shameful absurdities which still obstruct men's brains to such a degree as to make us doubt sometimes the possibility of a more human future.

Following on with the same order of protests against facts which have happened in history and of which consequently I myself recognise the inevitable character, I pause before the splendour of the Italian Republics and before the magnificent awakening of human genius in the epoch of the Renaissance. Then I see approaching the two evil geniuses, as ancient as history itself, the two boa-constrictors which up till now have devoured everything human and beautiful that history has produced. They are called the Church and the State, the Papacy and the Empire. Eternal evils and inseparable allies, I see them become reconciled, embrace each other and together devour and stifle and crush that unfortunate and too beautiful Italy, condemn her to three centuries of death. Well, again I find all that very natural, logical, inevitable, but nevertheless abominable, and I curse both Pope and Emperor at the same time.

Let us pass on to France. After a struggle which lasted a century, Catholicism, supported by the State, finally triumphed there over Protestantism. Well, do I not still find in France today some politicians or historians of the fatalist school and who, calling themselves Revolutionaries, consider this victory of Catholicism—a bloody and inhuman victory if ever there was one—as a veritable triumph for the Revolution? Catholicism, they maintain, was then the State, democracy, whilst Protestantism represented the revolt of the aristocracy against the State and consequently against democracy. It is with sophisms like that—completely identical besides with the Marxian sophisms, which, also, consider the triumphs of the State as those of Social Democracy—it is with these absurdities, as disgusting as revolting, that the mind and moral sense of the masses is perverted, habituating them to consider their blood-thirsty exploiters, their age-long enemies, their tyrants, the masters and the servants of the State, as the organs, representatives, heroes, devoted servants of their emancipation.

It is a thousand times right to say that Protestantism then, not as Calvinist theology, but as an energetic and armed protest, represented revolt, liberty, humanity, the destruction of the State; whilst Catholicism was public order, authority, divine law, the salvation of the State by the Church and the Church by the State, the condemnation of human society to a boundless and endless slavery.

Whilst recognising the inevitability of the accomplished fact, I do not hesitate to say that the triumph of Catholicism in France in the sixteenth and seventeenth centuries was a great misfortune for the whole human race, and that the massacre of Saint Bartholomew, as well as the Revocation of the Edict of Nantes, were facts as disastrous for France herself as were lately the defeat and massacre of the people of Paris in the Commune. I have actually heard very intelligent and very estimable Frenchmen explain this defeat of Protestantism in France by the essentially revolutionary nature of the French people. "Protestantism," they said, "was only a semi-revolution; we needed a complete revolution; it is for that reason that the French nation did not wish, and was not able, to stop at the Reformation. It preferred to remain Catholic till the moment when it could proclaim Atheism; and it is because of that that it bore with such a perfect and Christian resignation both the horrors of Saint Bartholomew and those not less abominable of the executors of the Revocation of the Edict of Nantes."

These estimable patriots do not seem to want to consider one thing. It is that a people who, under whatsoever pretext it may be, suffers tyranny, necessarily loses at length the salutory habit of revolt and even the very instinct of revolt. It loses the feeling for liberty, and once a people has lost all that, it necessarily becomes not only by its outer conditions, but in itself, in the very essence of its being, a people of slaves. It was because Protestantism was defeated in France that the French people lost, or rather never acquired, the custom of liberty. It is because this tradition and this custom are lacking in it that it has not today what we call political consciousness, and it is because it is lacking in this consciousness that all the revolutions it has made up to now have not been able to give it or secure it political liberty. With the exception of its great revolutionary days, which are its festival days, the French people remain today as yesterday, a people of slaves.

Chapter III; The State And Marxism

All work to be performed in the employ and pay of the State—such is the fundamental principle of Authoritarian Communism, of State Socialism. The State having become sole proprietor—at the end of a certain period of transition which will be necessary to let society pass without too great political and economic shocks from the present organisation of bourgeois privilege to the future organisation of the official equality of all—the State will be also the only Capitalist, banker, money-lender, organiser, director of all national labour and distributor of its products. Such is the ideal, the fundamental principle of modern Communism.

Enunciated for the first time by Babeuf towards the close of the Great French Revolution, with all the array of antique civism and revolutionary violence, which constituted the character of the epoch, it was recast and reproduced in miniature about forty-five years later by Louis Blanc in his tiny pamphlet on *The Organisation of Labour*, in which that estimable citizen, much less revolutionary and much more indulgent towards bourgeois weaknesses than was Babeuf, tried to gild and sweeten the pill so that the bourgeois could swallow it without suspecting that they were taking a poison which would kill them. But the bourgeois were not deceived, and returning brutality for politeness, they expelled Louis Blanc from France. In spite of that, with a constancy which one must admire, he remained alone in faithfulness to his economic system and continued to believe that the whole future was contained in his little pamphlet on the organisation of Labour.

The Communist idea later passed into more serious hands. Karl Marx, the undisputed chief of the Socialist Party in Germany—a great intellect armed with a profound knowledge, whose entire life, one can say it without flattering, has been devoted exclusively to the greatest cause which exists today, the emancipation of labour and of the toilers—Karl Marx who is indisputably also, if not the only, at least one of the principal founders of the International Workingmen's Association, made the development of the Communist idea the object of a serious work. His great work, *Capital*, is not in the least a fantasy, an "a priori" conception, hatched out in a single day in the head of a young man more or less ignorant of economic conditions and of the actual system of production. It is founded on a very extensive, very detailed knowledge and a very profound analysis of this system and of its conditions. Karl Marx is a man of immense statistical and economic knowledge. His work on Capital, though unfortunately bristling with formulas and metaphysical subtleties which render it unapproachable for the great mass of readers, is in the highest degree a scientific or realist work: in the sense that it absolutely excludes any other logic than that of the facts.

Living for very nearly thirty years almost exclusively among German workers, refugees like himself, and surrounded by more or less intelligent friends and disciples belonging by birth and relationship to the bourgeois world, Marx naturally has managed to form a Communist school, or a sort of little Communist Church, composed of fervent adepts and spread all over Germany. This Church, restricted though it may be on the score of numbers, is skillfully organised, and thanks to its numerous connections with working-class organisations in all the principal places in Germany, it has already become a power. Karl Marx naturally enjoys an almost supreme authority in this Church, and to do him justice, it must be admitted that he knows how to govern this little army of fanatical adherents in such a way as always to enhance his prestige and power over the imagination of the workers of Germany.

Marx is not only a learned Socialist, he is also a very clever Politician and an ardent patriot. Like Bismarck, though by somewhat different means, and like many other of his compatriots, Socialists or not, he wants the establishment of a great Germanic State for the glory of the German people and for the happiness and the voluntary, or enforced, civilization of the world.

The policy of Bismarck is that of the present; the policy of Marx, who considers himself at least as his successor, and his continuator, is that of the future. And when I say that Marx considers himself the continuator of Bismarck, I am far from calumniating Marx. If he did not consider himself as such, he would not have permitted Engels, the confidant of all his thoughts, to write that Bismarck serves the cause of Social Revolution. He serves it now in his own way; Marx will serve it later, in another manner. That is the sense in which he will be later the continuator, as today he is the admirer of the policy of Bismarck.

Now let us examine the particular character of Marx's policy, let us ascertain the essential points on which it is to be separated from the Bismarckian policy. The principal point, and, one might say, the only one, is this: Marx is a democrat, an Authoritarian Socialist, and a Republican; Bismarck is an out and out Pomeranian, aristocratic, monarchical Junker. The difference is therefore very great, very serious, and both sides are sincere in this difference. On this point, there is no possible understanding or reconciliation possible between Bismarck and Marx. Even apart from the numerous irrevocable pledges that Marx throughout his life has given to the cause of Socialist democracy, his very position and his ambitions give a positive guarantee on this issue. In a monarchy, however Liberal it might be, there cannot be any place, any role for Marx, and so much the more so in the Prussian Germanic Empire founded by Bismarck, with a bugbear of an Emperor, militarist and bigoted, as chief and with all the barons and bureaucrats of Germany for guardians. Before he can arrive at power, Marx will have to sweep all that away.

Therefore he is forced to be Revolutionary. That is what separates Marx from Bismarck — the form and the conditions of Government. One is an out and out aristocrat and monarchist;

and in a Conservative Republic like that of France under Thiers, there the other is an out and out democrat and republican, and, into the bargain, a Socialist democrat and a Socialist republican.

Let us see now what unites them. It is the out and out cult of the State. I have no need to prove it in the case of Bismarck, the proofs are there. From head to foot he is a State's man and nothing but a State's man. But neither do I believe that I shall have need of too great efforts to prove that it is the same with Marx. He loves government to such a degree that he even wanted to institute one in the International Workingmen's Association; and he worships power so much that he wanted to impose and still means today to impose his dictatorship on us. It seems to me that that is sufficient to characterise his personal attitude. But his Socialist and political programme is a very faithful expression of it. The supreme objective of all his efforts, as is proclaimed to us by the fundamental statutes of his party in Germany, is the establishment of the great People's State (*Volksstaat*).

But whoever says State, necessarily says a particular limited State, doubtless comprising, if it is very large, many different peoples and countries, but excluding still more. For unless he is dreaming of the Universal State as did Napoleon and the Emperor Charles the Fifth, or as the Papacy dreamed of the Universal Church, Marx, in spite of all the international ambition which devours him today, will have, when the hour of the realisation of his dreams has sounded for him—if it ever does sound—he will have to content himself with governing a single State and not several States at once. Consequently, who ever says State says, a State, and whoever says a State affirms by that the existence of several States, and whoever says several States, immediately says: competition, jealousy, truceless and endless war. The simplest logic as well as all history bear witness to it.

Any State, under pain of perishing and seeing itself devoured by neighbouring States, must tend towards complete power, and, having become powerful, it must embark on a career of conquest, so that it shall not be itself conquered; for two powers similar and at the same time foreign to each other could not co-exist without trying to destroy each other. Whoever says conquest, says conquered peoples, enslaved and in bondage, under whatever form or name it may be.

It is in the nature of the State to break the solidarity of the human race and, as it were, to deny humanity. The State cannot preserve itself as such in its integrity and in all its strength except it sets itself up as supreme and absolute be-all and end-all, at least for its own citizens, or to speak more frankly, for its own subjects, not being able to impose itself as such on the citizens of other States unconquered by it. From that there inevitably results a break with human, considered as universal, morality and with universal reason, by the birth of State morality and reasons of State. The principle of political or State morality is very simple. The State being the supreme objective, everything that is favourable to the development of its power is good; all that is contrary to it, even if it were the most humane thing in the world, is bad. This morality is called Patriotism. The International is the negation of patriotism and consequently the negation of the State. If therefore Marx and his friends of the German Socialist Democratic Party should succeed in introducing the State principle into our programme, they would kill the International.

The State, for its own preservation, must necessarily be powerful as regards foreign affairs; but if it is so as regards foreign affairs, it will infallibly be so as regards home affairs. Every State, having to let itself be inspired and directed by some particular morality, conformable to the particular conditions of its existence, by a morality which is a restriction and consequently a negation of human and universal morality, must keep watch that all its subjects, in their thoughts and above all in their acts, are inspired also only by the principles of this patriotic or particular morality, and that they remain deaf to the teachings of pure or universally human morality. From that there results the necessity for a State censorship; too great liberty of thought and opinions being, as Marx considers, very reasonably too from his eminently political point of view, incompatible with that unanimity of adherence demanded by the security of the State. That that in reality is Marx's opinion is sufficiently proved by the attempts which he made to introduce censorship into the International, under plausible pretexts, and covering it with a mask.

But however vigilant this censorship may be, even if the State were to take into its own hands exclusively education and all the instruction of the people, as Mazzini wished to do, and as Marx wishes to do today, the State can never be sure that prohibited and dangerous thoughts may not slip in and be smuggled somehow into the consciousness of the population that it governs. Forbidden fruit has such an attraction for men, and the demon of revolt, that eternal enemy of the State, awakens so easily in their hearts when they are not sufficiently stupified, that neither this education nor this instruction, nor even the censorship, sufficiently guarantee the tranquility of the State. It must still have a police, devoted agents who watch over and direct, secretly and unobtrusively, the current of the peoples' opinions and passions. We have seen that Marx himself is so convinced of this necessity, that he believed he should fill with his secret agents all the regions of the International and above all, Italy, France, and Spain. Finally, however perfect may be, from the point of view of the preservation of the State, the organsation of education and instruction for the people, of censorship and the police, the State cannot be secure in its existence while it does not have, to defend it against its enemies at home, an armed force. The State is government from above downwards of an immense number of men, very different from the point of view of the degree of their culture, the nature of the countries or localities that they inhabit, the occupation they follow, the interests and the aspirations directing them—the State is the government of all these by some or other minority; this minority, even if it were a thousand times elected by universal suffrage and controlled in its acts by popular institutions, unless it were endowed with the omniscience, omnipresence and the omnipotence which the theologians attribute to God, it is impossible that it could know and foresee the needs, or satisfy with an even justice the most legitimate and pressing interests in the world. There will always be discontented people because there will always be some who are sacrificed.

Besides, the State, like the Church, by its very nature is a great sacrificer of living beings. It is an arbitrary being, in whose heart all the positive, living, individual, and local interests of the population meet, clash, destroy each other, become absorbed in that abstraction called the common interest, the public good, the public safety, and where all real wills cancel each other in that other abstraction which hears the name of the will of the people. It results from this, that this so-called will of the people is never anything else than the sacrifice and the negation of all the real wills of the population; just as this so-called public good is nothing else than the sacrifice of their interests. But so that this omnivorous abstraction could impose itself on millions of men, it must be represented and supported by some real being, by living force or other. Well, this being, this force, has always existed. In the Church it is called the clergy, and in the State — the ruling or governing class.

And, in fact, what do we find throughout history? The State has always been the patrimony of some privileged class or other; a priestly class, an aristocratic class, a bourgeois class, and finally a bureaucratic class, when, all the other classes having become exhausted, the State falls or rises, as you will, to the condition of a machine; but it is absolutely necessary for the salvation of the State that there should be some privileged class or other which is interested in its existence. And it is precisely the united interest of this privileged class which is called Patriotism.

By excluding the immense majority of the human race from its bosom, by casting it beyond the pale of the engagements and reciprocal duties of morality, justice and right, the State denies humanity, and with that big word, "Patriotism", imposes injustice and cruelty on all its subjects, as a supreme duty. It restrains, it mutilates, it kills humanity in them, so that, ceasing to be men, they are no longer anything but citizens — or rather, more correctly considered in relation to the historic succession of facts — so that they shall never raise themselves beyond the level of the citizen to the level of a man.

If we accept the fiction of a free State derived from a social contract, then discerning, just, prudent people ought not to have any longer any need of government or of State. Such a people can need only to live, leaving a free course to all their instincts: justice and public order will naturally and of their accord proceed from the life of the people, and the State, ceasing to be the providence, guide, educator, and regulator of society, renouncing all its repressive power, and falling to the subaltern role which Proudhon assigns it, will no longer be anything else but a simple business office, a sort of central clearing house at the service of society.

Doubtless, such a political organisation, or rather, such a reduction of political action in favour of liberty in social life, would be a great benefit for society, but it would not at all please the devoted adherents of the State. They absolutely must have a State-Providence, a State directing social life, dispensing justice, and administering public order. That is to say, whether they admit it or not, and even when they call themselves Republicans, Democrats, or even Socialists, they always must have a people who are more or less ignorant, minor, incapable, or to call things by their right names, riff-raff, to govern; in order, of course, that, doing violence to their own disinterestedness and modesty, they can keep the best places for themselves, in order always to have the opportunity to devote themselves to the common good, and that, strong in their virtuous devotion and their exclusive intelligence, privileged guardians of the human flock, whilst urging it on for its own good and leading it to security, they may also fleece it a little.

Every logical and sincere theory of the State is essentially founded on the principle of authority—that is to say on the eminently theological, metaphysical and political idea that the masses, always incapable of governing themselves, must submit at all times to the benevolent yoke of a wisdom and a justice, which in one way or another is imposed on them from above. But imposed in the name of what and by whom? Authority recognised and respected as such by the masses can have only three possible sources—force, religion, or the action of a superior intelligence; and this supreme intelligence is always represented by minorities.

Slavery can change its form and its name—its basis remains the same. This basis is expressed by the words: being a slave is being forced to work for other people—as being a master is to live on the labour of other people. In ancient times, as today in Asia and Africa, slaves were simply called slaves. In the Middle Ages, they took the name of "serfs", today they are called "wage-earners". The position of these latter is much more honourable and less hard than that of slaves, but they are none the less forced, by hunger as well as by the political and social institutions, to maintain by very hard work the absolute or relative idleness of others. Consequently, they are slaves. And, in general, no State, either ancient or modern, has ever been able, or ever will be able, to do without the forced labour of the masses, whether wage-earners or slaves, as a principal and absolutely necessary basis of the liberty and culture of the political class: the citizens.

Even the United States is no exception to this rule. Its marvelous prosperity and enviable progress are due in great part and above all to one important advantage—the great territorial wealth of North America. The immense quantity of uncultivated and fertile lands, together with a political liberty that exists nowhere else, attracts every year hundreds of thousands of energetic, industrious and intelligent colonists. This wealth at the same time keeps off pauperism and delays the moment when the social question will have to be put. A worker who does not find work or who is dissatisfied with the wages offered by the capitalist can always, if need be, emigrate to the far West to clear there some wild and unoccupied land.

This possibility, always remaining open as a last resort to all American workers, naturally keeps wages at a level, and gives to every individual an independence, unknown in Europe. Such is the advantage, but here is the disadvantage. As cheapness of the products of industry is achieved in great part by cheapness of labour, the American manufacturers for most of the time are not in a condition to compete against the manufacturers of Europe—from which there results, for the industry of the Northern States, the necessity for a protectionist tariff. But that has a result, firstly to create a host of artificial industries and above all to oppress and ruin the non-manufacturing Southern States and make them want secession; finally to crowd together into cities like New York, Philadelphia, Boston and many others, proletarian working masses who, little by little, are beginning to find themselves already in a situation analogous to that of the workers in the great manufacturing States of Europe. And we see in effect the social question already being posed in the Northern States, just as it was posed long before in our countries.

And there too, the self-government of the masses, in spite of all the display of the people's omnipotence, remains most of the time in a state of fiction. In reality, it is minorities which govern. The so-called Democratic Party, up to the time of the Civil War to emancipate the slaves, were the out and out partisans of slavery and of the ferocious oligarchy of the planters, demagogues without faith or conscience, capable of sacrificing everything to their greed and evil-minded ambition, and who, by their detestable influence and actions, exercised almost unhindered, for nearly fifty years continuously, have greatly contributed to deprave the political morality of North America.

The Republican Party, though really intelligent and generous, is still and always a minority, and whatever the sincerity of this party of liberation, however great and generous the principles it professes, do not let us hope that, in power, it will renounce this exclusive position of a governing minority to merge into the mass of the nation so that the self-government of the people shall finally become a reality. For that there will be necessary a revolution far more profound than all those which hitherto have shaken the Old and New Worlds.

In Switzerland, in spite of all the democratic revolutions that have taken place there, it is still always the class in comfortable circumstances, the bourgeoisie, that is to say, the class privileged by wealth, leisure, and education, which governs. The sovereignty of the people—a word which, anyway, we detest because in our eyes, all sovereignty is detestable—the government of the people by themselves is likewise a fiction. The people is sovereign in law, not in fact, for necessarily absorbed by their daily labour, which leaves them no leisure, and if not completely ignorant, at least very inferior in education to the bourgeoisie, they are forced to place in the hands of the latter their supposed sovereignty. The sole advantage which they get out of it in Switzerland, as in the United States, is that ambitious minorities, the political classes, cannot arrive at power otherwise than by paying court to the people, flattering their fleeting passions, which may sometimes be very bad, and most often deceiving them.

It is true that the most imperfect republic is a thousand times better than the most enlightened monarchy, for at least in the republic there are moments when, though always exploited, the people are not oppressed, while in monarchies they are never anything else. And then the democratic regime trains the masses little by little in public life, which the monarchy never does. But whilst giving the preference to the republic we are nevertheless forced to recognise and proclaim that whatever may be the form of government, whilst human society remains divided into different classes because of the hereditary inequality of occupations, wealth, education, and privileges, there will always be minority government and the inevitable exploitation of the majority by that minority.

The State is nothing else but this domination and exploitation regularised and systematised. We shall attempt to demonstrate it by examining the consequence of the government of the masses of the people by a minority, at first as intelligent and as devoted as you like, in an ideal State, founded on a free contract.

Suppose the government to be confined only to the best citizens. At first these citizens are privileged not by right, but by fact. They have been elected by the people because they are the most intelligent, clever, wise, and courageous and devoted. Taken from the mass of the citizens, who are regarded as all equal, they do not yet form a class apart, but a group of men privileged only by nature and for that very reason singled out for election by the people. Their number is necessarily very limited, for in all times and countries the number of men endowed with qualities so remarkable that they automatically command the unanimous respect of a nation is, as experience teaches us, very small. Therefore, under pain of making a bad choice, the people will be always forced to choose its rulers from amongst them.

Here, then, is society divided into two categories, if not yet to say two classes, of which one, composed of the immense majority of the citizens, submits freely to the government of its elected leaders, the other, formed of a small number of privileged natures, recognised and accepted as such by the people, and charged by them to govern them. Dependent on popular election, they are at first distinguished from the mass of the citizens only by the very qualities which recommended them to their choice and are, naturally, the most devoted and useful of all. They do not yet assume to themselves any privilege, any particular right, except that of exercising, insofar as the people wish it, the special functions with which they have been charged. For the rest, by their manner of life, by the conditions and means of their existence, they do not separate themselves in any way from all the others, so that a perfect equality continues to reign among all. Can this equality be long maintained? We claim that it cannot and nothing is easier to prove it.

Nothing is more dangerous for man's private morality than the habit of command. The best man, the most intelligent, disinterested, generous, pure, will infallibly and always be spoiled at this trade. Two sentiments inherent in power never fail to produce this demoralisation; they are: contempt for the masses, and the overestimation of one's own merits.

"The masses," a man says to himself, "recognising their incapacity to govern on their own account, have elected me their chief. By that act they have publicly proclaimed their inferiority and my superiority. Among this crowd of men, recognising hardly any equals of myself, I am alone capable of directing public affairs. The people have need of me; they cannot do without my services, while I, on the contrary, can get along all right by myself: they, therefore, must obey me for their own security, and in condescending to command them, I am doing them a good turn."

Is not there something in all that to make a man lose his head and his heart as well, and become mad with pride? It is thus that power and the habit of command become for even the most intelligent and virtuous men, a source of aberration, both intellectual and moral.

But in the People's State of Marx, there will be, we are told, no privileged class at all. All will be equal, not only from the juridical and political point of view, but from the economic point of view. At least that is what is promised, though I doubt very much, considering the manner in which it is being tackled and the course it is desired to follow, whether that promise could ever be kept. There will therefore be no longer any privileged class, but there will be a government and, note this well, an extremely complex government, which will not content itself with governing and administering the masses politically, as all governments do today, but which will also administer them economically, concentrating in its own hands the production and the just division of wealth, the cultivation of land, the establishment and development of factories, the organisation and direction of commerce, finally the application of capital to production by the only banker, the State. All that will demand an immense knowledge and many "heads overflowing with brains" in this government. It will be the reign of scientific intelligence, the most aristocratic, despotic, arrogant and contemptuous of all regimes. There will be a new class, a new hierarchy of real and pretended scientists and scholars, and the world will be divided into a minority ruling in the name of knowledge and an immense ignorant majority. And then, woe betide the mass of ignorant ones!

Such a regime will not fail to arouse very considerable discontent in this mass and in order to keep it in check the enlightenment and liberating government of Marx will have need of a not less considerable armed force. For the government must be strong, says Engels, to maintain order among these millions of illiterates whose brutal uprising would be capable of destroying and overthrowing everything, even a government directed by heads overflowing with brains.

You can see quite well that behind all the democratic and socialistic phrases and promises of Marx's programme, there is to be found in his State all that constitutes the true despotic and brutal nature of all States, whatever may be the form of their government and that in the final reckoning, the People's State so strongly commended by Marx, and the aristocratic-monarchic State, maintained with as much cleverness as power by Bismarck, are completely identical by the nature of their objective at home as well as in foreign affairs. In foreign affairs it is the same deployment of military force, that is to say, conquest; and in home affairs it is the same employment of this armed force, the last argument of all threatened political powers against the masses, who, tired of believing, hoping, submitting and obeying always, rise in revolt.

Marx's Communist idea comes to light in all his writings; it is also manifest in the motions put forward by the General Council of the International Workingmen's Association, situated in London, at the Congress of Basel in 1869, as well as by the proposals which he had intended to present to the Congress which was to take place in September, 1870, but which had to be suspended because of the Franco-German War. As a member of the General Council in London and as corresponding Secretary for Germany, Marx enjoys in this Council, as is well known, a great and, it must be admitted, legitimate influence, so that it can be taken for certain that of the motions put to the Congress by the Council, several are principally derived from the system and the collaboration of Marx. It was in this way that the English citizen Lucraft, a member of the General Council, put forward at the Congress of Basel the idea that all the land in a country should become the property of the State, and that the cultivation of this land should be directed and administered by State officials, "Which," he added, "will only be possible in a democratic and Socialist State, in which the people will have to watch carefully over the good administration of the national land by the State."

This cult of the State is, in general, the principal characteristic of German Socialism. Lassalle, the greatest Socialist agitator and the true founder of the practical Socialist movement in Germany, was steeped in it. He saw no salvation for the workers except in the power of the State; of which the workers should possess themselves, according to him, by means of universal suffrage.

Chapter IV; Internationalism And The State

Let us consider the real, national policy of Marx himself. Like Bismarck, he is a German patriot. He desires the greatness and power of Germany as a State. No one anyway will count it a crime in him to love his country and his people; and since he is so profoundly convinced that the State is the condition *sine qua non* of the prosperity of the one and the emancipation of the other, it will be found natural that he should desire to see Germany organized into a very large and very powerful State, since weak and small States always run the risk of seeing themselves swallowed up. Consequently Marx, as a clear-sighted and ardent patriot, must wish for the greatness and strength of Germany as a State.

But, on the other hand, Marx is a celebrated Socialist and, what is more, one of the principal initiators of the International. He does not content himself with working for the emancipation of the proletariat of Germany alone; he feels himself in honor bound, and he considers it as his duty, to work at the same time for the emancipation of the proletariat of all other countries; the result is that he finds himself in complete conflict with himself. As a German patriot, he wants the greatness and power, that is to say, the domination of Germany; but as a Socialist of the International he must wish for the emancipation of all the peoples of the world. How can this contradiction be resolved?

There is only one way, that is to proclaim, after he has persuaded himself of it, of course, that the greatness and power of Germany as a State is a supreme condition of the emancipation of the whole world, that the national and political triumph of Germany is the triumph of humanity, and that all that is contrary to the advent of this great new omnivorous power is the enemy of humanity. This conviction once established, it is not only permitted, but it is commanded by the most sacred of causes, to make the International, including all the Federations of other countries, serve as a very powerful, convenient, above all, popular means for the setting up of the great Pan-German State. And that is precisely what Marx tried to do, as much by the deliberations of the Conference he called at London in 1871 as by the resolutions voted by his German and French friends at the Hague Congress. If he did not succeed better, it is assuredly not for lack of very great efforts and much skill on his part, but probably because the fundamental idea which inspires him is false and its realization is impossible.

One cannot commit a greater mistake than to ask either of a thing or of an institution or of a man more than they can give. By demanding more from them one demoralises, impedes, perverts and kills them. The International in a short time produced great results. It organised and it will organise every day in a more formidable manner still, the proletariat for the economic struggle. Is that a reason to hope that one can use it as an instrument for the political struggle? Marx, because he thought so, very nearly killed the International, by his criminal attempt at The Hague. It is the story of the goose with the golden eggs. At the summons to the economic struggle, masses of workers of different countries hastened along to range themselves under the flag of the International, and Marx imagined that the masses would stay under it—what do I say?—that they would hasten along in still more formidable numbers, when he, a new Moses, had inscribed the maxims of his political decalogue on our flag in the official and binding programme of the International.

There his mistake lay. The masses, without distinction of degree of culture, religious beliefs, country and speech, had understood the language of the International when it spoke to them of their poverty, their sufferings and their slavery under the yoke of Capitalism and exploiting private ownership; they understood it when it demonstrated to them the necessity of uniting their efforts in a great solid, common struggle. But here they were being talked to about a very learned and above all very authoritarian political programme, which, in the name of their own salvation, was attempting, in that very International which was to organise their emancipation by their own efforts, to impose on them a dictatorial government, provisional, no doubt, but, meanwhile, completely arbitrary and directed by a head extraordinarily filled with brains.

Marx's programme is a complete fabric of political and economic institutions, strongly centralised and very authoritarian, sanctioned, no doubt, like all despotic institutions in modern society, by universal suffrage, but subordinate nevertheless to a very strong government; to use the very words of Engels, the alter ego of Marx, the confidant of the legislator.

To what a degree of madness would not one have to be driven by ambition, or vanity, or both at once, to have been capable of conceiving the hope that one could retain the working masses of the different countries of Europe and America under the flag of the International on these conditions!

A universal State, government, dictatorship! The dream of Popes Gregory VII and Boniface VIII, of the Emperor Charles V, and of Napoleon, reproducing itself under new forms, but always with the same pretensions in the camp of Socialist Democracy! Can one imagine anything more burlesque, but also anything more revolting?

To maintain that one group of individuals, even the most intelligent and the best intentioned, are capable of becoming the thought, the soul, the guiding and unifying will of the revolutionary movement and of the economic organisation of the proletariat in all countries, is such a heresy against common sense, and against the experience of history, that one asks oneself with astonishment how a man as intelligent as Marx could have conceived it.

The Pope had at least for an excuse the absolute truth which they claimed rested in their hands by the grace of the Holy Spirit and in which they were supposed to believe. Marx has not this excuse, and I shall not insult him by thinking that he believes himself to have scientifically invented something which approaches absolute truth. But from the moment that the absolute does not exist, there cannot be any infallible dogma for the International, nor consequently any official political and economic theory, and our Congresses must never claim the role of General Church Councils, proclaiming obligatory principles for all adherents and believers. There exists only one law which is really obligatory for all members, individual sections and federations in the International, of which this law constitutes the true and only basis. It is, in all its extension, in all its consequences and applications — the International solidarity of the toilers in all trades and in all countries in their economic struggle against the exploiters of labour. It is in the real organisation of this solidarity, by the spontaneous organisation of the working masses and by the absolutely free federation, powerful in proportion as it will be free, of the working masses of all languages and nations, and not in their unification by decrees and under the rod of any government whatever, that there resides the real and living unity of the International. That from this ever broader organisation of the militant solidarity of the proletariat against bourgeois exploitation there must issue, and in fact there does arise, the political struggle of the proletariat against the bourgeoisie; who can doubt? The Marxians and ourselves are unanimous on this point. But immediately there presents itself the question which separates us so profoundly from the Marxians.

We think that the necessarily revolutionary policy of the proletariat must have for its immediate and only object the destruction of States. We do not understand that anyone could speak of international solidarity when they want to keep States—unless they are dreaming of the Universal State, that is to say, universal slavery like the great Emperors and Popes— the State by its very nature being a rupture of this solidarity and consequently a permanent cause of war. Neither do we understand how anybody could speak of the freedom of the proletariat or of the real deliverance of the masses in the State and by the State. State means domination, and all domination presupposes the subjection of the masses and consequently their exploitation to the profit of some minority or other.

We do not admit, even as a revolutionary transition, either National Conventions, or Constituent Assemblies, or so-called revolutionary dictatorships; because we are convinced that the revolutionary is only sincere, honest and real in the masses, and that when it is concentrated in the hands of some governing individuals, it naturally and inevitably becomes reaction.

The Marxians profess quite contrary ideas. As befits good Germans, they are worshipers of the power of the State, and necessarily also the prophets of political and social discipline, the champions of order established from above downwards, always in the name of universal suffrage and the sovereignty of the masses, to whom they reserve the happiness and honour of obeying chiefs, elected masters. The Marxians admit no other emancipation than that which they expect from their so-called People's States. They are so little the enemies of patriotism that their International, even, wears too often the colours of Pan-Germanism. Between the Marxian policy and the Bismarckian policy there no doubt exists a very appreciable difference, but between the Marxians and ourselves, there is an abyss. They are Governmentalists, we are out and out Anarchists.

Indeed, between these two tendencies no conciliation today is possible. Only the practical experience of social revolution, of great new historic experiences, the logic of events, can bring them sooner or later to a common solution; and strongly convinced of the rightness of our principle, we hope that then the Germans themselves—the workers of Germany and not their leaders—will finish by joining us in order to demolish those prisons of peoples, that are called States and to condemn politics, which indeed is nothing but the art of dominating and fleecing the masses.

At a pinch I can conceive that despots, crowned or uncrowned, could dream of the sceptre of the world; but what can be said of a friend of the proletariat, of a revolutionary who seriously claims that he desires the emancipation of the masses and who setting himself up as director and supreme arbiter of all the revolutionary movements which can burst forth in different countries, dares to dream of the subjection of the proletariat of all these countries to a single thought, hatched in his own brain.

I consider that Marx is a very serious revolutionary, if not always a very sincere one, and that he really wants to uplift the masses, and I ask myself—Why it is that he does not perceive that the establishment of a universal dictatorship, whether collective or individual, of a dictatorship which would perform in some degree the task of chief engineer of the world revolution—ruling and directing the insurrectional movement of the masses in all countries as one guides a machine—that the establishment of such a dictatorship would suffice by itself alone to kill the revolution, or paralyse and pervert all the people's movements? What is the man, what is the group of individuals, however great may be their genius, who would dare to flatter themselves to be able to embrace and comprehend the infinite multitude of interests, of tendencies and actions, so diverse in each country, province, locality, trade, and of which the immense totality, united, but not made uniform, by one grand common aspiration and by some fundamental principles which have passed henceforth into the consciousness of the masses, will constitute the future social revolution?

And what is to be thought of an International Congress which in the so-called interests of this revolution, imposes on the proletariat of the whole civilised world a government invested with dictatorial power, with the inquisitorial and dictatorial rights of suspending regional federations, of proclaiming a ban against whole nations in the name of a so-called official principle, which is nothing else than Marx's own opinion, transformed by the vote of a fake majority into an absolute truth? What is to be thought of a Congress which, doubtless to render its folly still more patent, relegates to America this dictatorial governing body, after having composed it of men probably very honest, but obscure, sufficiently ignorant, and absolutely unknown to it. Our enemies the bourgeois would then be right when they laugh at our Congresses and when they claim that the International only fights old tyrannies in order to establish new ones, and that in order worthily to replace existing absurdities, it wishes to create another!

Chapter V; Social Revolution And The State

What Bismarck has done for the political and bourgeois world, Marx claims to do today for the Socialist world, among the proletariat of Europe; to replace French initiative by German initiative and domination; and as, according to him and his disciples, there is no German thought more advanced than his own, he believed the moment had come to have it triumph theoretically and practically in the International. Such was the only object of the Conference which he called together in September 1871 in London. This Marxian thought is explicitly developed in the famous *Manifesto* of the refugee German Communists drafted and published in 1848 by Marx and Engels. It is the theory of the emancipation of the proletariat and of the organisation of labour by the State.

Its principal point is the conquest of political power by the working class. One can understand that men as indispensable as Marx and Engels should be the partisans of a programme which, consecrating and approving political power, opens the door to all ambitions. Since there will be political power there will necessarily be subjects, got up in Republican fashion as citizens, it is true, but who will none the less be subjects, and who as such will be forced to obey — because without obedience, there is no power possible. It will be said in answer to this that they will obey not men but laws which they will have made themselves. To that I shall reply that everybody knows how much, in the countries which are freest and most democratic, but politically governed, the people make the laws, and what their obedience to these laws signifies. Whoever is not deliberately desirous of taking fictions for realities must recognise quite well that, even in such countries, the people really obey not laws which they make themselves, but laws which are made in their name, and that to obey these laws means nothing else to them than to submit to the arbitrary will of some guarding and governing minority or, what amounts to the same thing, to be freely slaves.

There is in this programme another expression which is profoundly antipathetic to us revolutionary Anarchists who frankly want the complete emancipation of the people; the expression to which I refer is the presentation of the proletariat, the whole society of toilers, as a "class" and not as a "mass". Do you know what that means? Neither more nor less than a new aristocracy, that of the workers of the factories and towns, to the exclusion of the millions who constitute the proletariat of the countryside and who in the anticipations of the Social Democrats of Germany will, in effect, become subjects of their great so-called People's State. "Class", "Power", "State", are three inseparable terms, of which each necessarily pre-supposes the two others and which all definitely are to be summed up by the words: the political subjection and the economic exploitation of the masses.

The Marxians think that just as in the 18th Century the bourgeoisie dethroned the nobility, to take its place and to absorb it slowly into its own body, sharing with it the domination and exploitation of the toilers in the towns as well as in the country, so the proletariat of the towns is called on today to dethrone the bourgeoisie, to absorb it and to share with it the domination and exploitation of the proletariat of the countryside; this last outcast of history, unless this latter later revolts and demolishes all classes, denominations, powers, in a word, all States.

To me, however, the flower of the proletariat does not mean, as it does to the Marxians, the upper layer, the most civilised and comfortably off in the working world, that layer of semi-bourgeois workers, which is precisely the class the Marxians want to use to constitute their fourth governing class, and which is really capable of forming one if things are not set to rights in the interests of the great mass of the proletariat; for with its relative comfort and semi-bourgeois position, this upper layer of workers is unfortunately only too deeply penetrated with all the political and social prejudices and all the narrow aspirations and pretensions of the bourgeois. It can be truly said that this upper layer is the least socialist, the most individualist in all the proletariat.

By the flower of the proletariat, I mean above all that great mass, those millions of non-civilised, disinherited, wretched and illiterates whom Messrs. Engels and Marx mean to subject to the paternal regime of a very strong government, to employ an expression used by Engels in a letter to our friend Cafiero. Without doubt, this will be for their own salvation, as of course all governments, as is well known, have been established solely in the interests of the masses themselves. By the flower of the proletariat I mean precisely that eternal "meat" for governments, that great rabble of the people ordinarily designated by Messrs. Marx and Engels by the phrase at once picturesque and contemptuous of "*lumpen proletariat*", the "riff raff", that rabble which, being very nearly unpolluted by all bourgeois civilization, carries in its heart, in its aspirations, in all necessities and the miseries of its collective position, all the germs of the Socialism of the future, and which alone is powerful enough today to inaugurate the Social Revolution and bring it to triumph.

Though differing from us in this respect also, the Marxians do not reject our programme absolutely. They only reproach us with wanting to hasten, to outstrip, the slow march of history and to ignore the scientific law of successive evolutions. Having had the thoroughly German nerve to proclaim in their worlds consecrated to the philosophical analysis of the past that the bloody defeat of the insurgent peasants of Germany and the triumph of the despotic States in the sixteenth century constituted a great revolutionary progress, they today have the nerve to satisfy themselves with establishing a new despotism to the so-called profit of the town-workers and to the detriment of the toilers in the country.

To support his programme of the conquest of political power, Marx has a very special theory which is, moreover, only a logical consequence of his whole system. The political condition of each country, says he, is always the product and the faithful expression of its economic situation; to change the former it is only necessary to transform the latter. According to Marx, all the secret of historic evolution is there. He takes no account of other elements in history, such as the quite obvious reaction of political, juridical, and religious institutions on the economic situation. He says, "Poverty produces political slavery, the State," but he does not allow this expression to be turned around to say "Political slavery, the State, reproduces in its turn, and maintains poverty as a condition of its own existence; so that, in order to destroy poverty, it is necessary to destroy the State!" And, a strange thing in him who forbids his opponents to lay the blame on political slavery, the State, as an active cause of poverty, he commands his friends and disciples of the Social Democratic Party in Germany to consider the conquest of power and of political liberties as the preliminary condition absolutely necessary for economic emancipation.

Yet the sociologists of the school of Marx, men like Engels and Lassalle, object against us that the State is not at all the cause of the poverty of the people, of the degradation and servitude of the masses; but that the wretched condition of the masses, as well as the despotic power of the State are, on the contrary, both the one and the other, the effects of a more general cause, the products of an inevitable phase in the economic development of society, of a phase which, from the point of view of history, constitutes true progress, an immense step towards what they call the social revolution. To such a degree, in fact, that Lassalle did not hesitate loudly to proclaim that the defeat of the formidable revolt of the peasants in Germany in the sixteenth century—a deplorable defeat if ever there was one, from which dates the centuries-old slavery of the Germans, and the triumph of the despotic and centralised State which was the necessary consequence of it—constituted a real triumph for this revolution; because the peasants, say the Marxians, are the natural representatives of reaction, whilst the modern military and bureaucratic State—a product and inevitable accompaniment of the social revolution, which, starting from the second half of the sixteenth century commenced the slow, but always progressive transformation of the ancient feudal and land economy into the production of wealth, or, what comes to the same thing, into the exploitation of the labour of the people by capital—this State was an essential condition of this revolution.

One can understand how Engels, driven on by the same logic, in a letter addressed to one of our friends, Carlo Cafiero, was able to say, without the least irony, but on the contrary, very seriously, that Bismarck as well as King Victor Emmanuel II had rendered immense services to the revolution, both of them having created political centralisation in their respective countries.

Likewise Marx completely ignores a most important element in the historic development of humanity, that is, the temperament and particular character of each race and each people, a temperament and character which are naturally themselves the product of a multitude of ethnographical, climatological, economic, as well as historic causes, but which, once produced, exercise, even apart from and independent of the economic conditions of each country, a considerable influence on its destinies, and even on the development of its economic forces. Among these elements and these so to say natural traits, there is one whose action is completely decisive in the particular history of each people; it is the intensity of the instinct of revolt, and by the same token, of liberty, with which it is endowed or which is has conserved. This instinct is a fact which is completely primordial and animal; one finds it in different degrees in every living being, and the energy, the vital power of each, is to be measured by its intensity. In man, besides the economic needs which urge him on, this instinct becomes the most powerful agent of all human emancipations. And as it is a matter of temperament, not of intellectual and moral culture, although ordinarily it evokes one and the other, it sometimes happens that civilised peoples possess it only in a feeble degree, whether it is that it has been exhausted during their previous development, or whether the very nature of their civilisation has depraved them, or whether, finally, they were originally less endowed with it than were others.

Such has been in all its past, such is still today the Germany of the nobles and the bourgeoisie. The German proletariat, a victim for centuries of one and the other, can it be made jointly responsible for the spirit of conquest which manifests itself today in the upper classes of this nation? In actual fact, undoubtedly, no. For a conquering people is necessarily a slave people, and the slaves are always the proletariat. Conquest is therefore completely opposed to their interests and liberty. But they are jointly responsible for it in spirit, and they will remain jointly responsible as long as they do not understand that this Pan-German State, this Republican and so-called People's State, which is promised them in a more or less near future, would be nothing else, if it could ever be realised, than a new form of very hard slavery for the proletariat.

Up to the present, at least, they do not seem to have understood it, and none of their chiefs, orators, or publicists has given himself the trouble to explain it to them. They are all trying, on the contrary, to inveigle the proletariat along a path where they will meet with nothing but the adversion of the world and their own enslavement; and, as long as, obeying the directions of these leaders, they pursue this frightful illusion of a People's State, certainly the proletariat will not have the initiative for social revolution. This Revolution will come to it from outside, probably from the Mediterranean countries, and then yielding to the universal contagion, the German proletariat will unloose its passions and will overthrow at one stroke the dominion of its tyrants and of its so-called emancipation.

The reasoning of Marx leads to absolutely opposite results. Taking into consideration nothing but the one economic question, he says to himself that the most advanced countries and consequently the most capable of making a social revolution, are those in which modern Capitalist production has reached its highest degree of development. It is they that, to the exclusion of all others, are the civilised countries, the only ones called on to initiate and direct this revolution. This revolution will consist in the expropriation, whether by peaceful succession or by violence, of the present property-owners and capitalists and in the appropriation of all lands and all capital by the State, which in order to fulfill its great economic as well as political mission must necessarily be very powerful and very strongly centralised. The State will administer and direct the cultivation of the land by means of its salaried officers, commanding armies of rural toilers, organised and disciplined for this cultivation. At the same time, on the ruin of all the existing banks it will establish a single bank, financing all labour and all national commerce.

One can understand that, at first sight, such a simple plan of organisation—at least in appearance—could seduce the imagination of workers more eager for justice and equality than for liberty, and foolishly fancying that these two can exist without liberty—as if to gain and consolidate justice and equality, one could rely on other people, and on ruling groups above all, however much they may claim to be elected and controlled by the people. In reality it would be for the proletariat a barrack regime, where the standardised mass of men and women workers would wake, sleep, work and live to the beat of the drum; for the clever and the learned a privilege of governing; and for the mercenary minded, attracted by the immensity of the international speculations of the national banks, a vast field of lucrative jobbery.

At home it will be slavery, in foreign affairs a truceless war; unless all the peoples of the "inferior" races, Latin or Slav, the one tired of the bourgeois civilisation, the other almost ignorant of it and despising it by instinct, unless these peoples resign themselves to submit to the yoke of an essentially bourgeois nation and a State all the more despotic because it will call itself the People's State.

The social revolution, as the Latin and Slav toilers picture it to themselves, desire it and hope for it, is infinitely broader than that promised them by the German or Marxian programme. It is not for them a question of the emancipation parsimoniously measured out and only realisable at a very distant date, of the working class, but the complete and real emancipation of all the proletariat, not only of some countries but of all nations, civilised and uncivilised — a new civilisation, genuinely of the people, being destined to commence by this act of universal emancipation.

And the first word of this emancipation can be none other than "Liberty", not that political, bourgeois liberty, so much approved and recommended as a preliminary object of conquest by Marx and his adherents, but the great human liberty which, destroying all the dogmatic, metaphysical, political and juridical fetters by which everybody today is loaded down, will give to everybody, collectivities as well as individuals, full autonomy in their activities and their development, delivered once and for all from all inspectors, directors and guardians.

The second word of this emancipation is "Solidarity", not the Marxian solidarity from above downwards by some government or other, either by ruse or by force, on the masses of the people; not that solidarity of all which is the negation of the liberty of each, and which by that very fact becomes a falsehood, a fiction, having slavery as the reality behind it; but that solidarity which is on the contrary the confirmation and the realisation of every liberty, having its origin not in any political law whatsoever, but in the inherent collective nature of man, in virtue of which no man is free if all the men who surround him and who exercise the least influence, direct or indirect, on his life are not so equally. This truth is to be found magnificently expressed in the Declaration of the Rights of Man drafted by Robespierre, and which proclaims that the slavery of the least of men is the slavery of all.

The solidarity which we ask, far from being the result of any artificial or authoritarian organisation whatsoever, can only be the spontaneous product of social life, economic as well as moral; the result of the free federation of common interests, aspirations and tendencies. It has for essential bases, equality, collective labour — becoming obligatory for each not by the force of law, but by the force of facts—and collective property as a directing light, experience—that is to say the practice of the collective life; knowledge and learning; and as a final goal the establishment of Humanity, and consequently the ruin of all States.

There is the ideal, not divine, not metaphysical, but human and practical, which alone corresponds to the modern aspirations of the Latin and Slav peoples. They want complete liberty, complete solidarity, complete equality; in a word, they want only Humanity and they will not be satisfied, even on the score of its being provisional and transitory, with anything less than that. The Marxians will denounce their aspirations as folly; that has been done over a long period, that has not turned them from their goal, and they will never change the magnificence of that goal for the completely bourgeois platitudes of Marxian Socialism.

Their ideal is practical in this sense, that its realisation will be much less difficult than that of the Marxian idea, which, besides the poverty of its objective, presents also the grave inconvenience of being absolutely impracticable. It will not be the first time that clever men, rational and advocates of things practical and possible, will be recognised for Utopians, and that those who are called Utopians today will be recognised as practical men tomorrow. The absurdity of the Marxian system consists precisely in the hope that by inordinately narrowing down the Socialist programme so as to make it acceptable to the bourgeois Radicals, it will transform the latter into unwitting and involuntary servants of the social revolution. There is a great error there; all the experience of history demonstrates to us that an alliance concluded between two different parties always turns to the advantage of the more reactionary of the two parties; this alliance necessarily enfeebles the more progressive party, by diminishing and distorting its programme, by destroying its moral strength, its confidence in itself, whilst a reactionary party, when it is guilty of falsehood is always and more than ever true to itself.

As for me, I do not hesitate to say that all the Marxist flirtations with the Radicalism, whether reformist or revolutionary, of the bourgeois, can have no other result than the demoralisation and disorganisation of the rising power of the proletariat, and consequently a new consolidation of the established power of the bourgeois.

Chapter VI; Political Action And The Workers

In Germany, Socialism is already beginning to be a formidable power, despite restrictive and oppressive laws. The workers' parties are frankly Socialist—in the sense that they want a Socialistic reform of the relations between capital and labour, and that they consider that to obtain this reform, the State must first of all be reformed, and that if it will not suffer itself to be reformed peaceably, it must be reformed by political revolution. This political revolution, they maintain, must precede the social revolution, but I consider this a fatal error, as such a revolution would necessarily be a bourgeois revolution and would produce only a bourgeois socialism, that is to say it would lead to a new exploitation, more cunning and hypocritical, but not less oppressive than the present.

This idea of a political revolution preceding a social revolution has opened wide the doors of the Social Democratic Party to all the Radical democrats; who are very little Socialists. And the leaders of the Party have, against the instincts of the workers themselves, brought into close association with the bourgeois democrats of the People's Party, which is quite hostile to Socialism, as its Press and politicians demonstrate. The leaders of this People's party, however, have observed that these anti-Socialist utterances displeased the workers, and they modified the tone for they need the workers' assistance in their political aims, just as it has always been the all-powerful arm of the people and then filch the profits for themselves. Thus these Popular democrats have now become "Socialists" of a sort. But the "Socialism" does not go beyond the harmless dreams of bourgeois co-operativism.

At a Congress in Eisenach, in August, 1869, there were negotiations between the representatives of the two parties, worker and democrat, and these resulted in a programme which definitely constituted the Social Democratic Labour Party. This programme is a compromise between the Socialist and revolutionary progamme of the International as determined by the Congresses of Brussels and Basel, and the programme of bourgeois democracy. This new programme called for a "free People's State", wherein all class domination and all exploitation would be abolished. Political liberty was declared to be the most urgently needed condition for the economic emancipation of the working classes. Consequently the social question was inseparable from the political question. Its solution was possible only in a democratic State. The Party was declared to be associated with the International. Some immediate objectives were set out: manhood suffrage, referenda, free and compulsory education, separation of Church and State, liberty of the Press, State aid to workers' co-operatives.

This programme expresses not the Socialist and revolutionary aspirations of the workers, but the policy of the leaders. There is a direct contradiction between the programme of the International, and the purely national programme set out above, between the socialist solidarity of Labour and the political patriotism of the National State. Thus the Social Democrats find themselves in the position of being united with their bourgeois compatriots against the workers of a foreign country; and their patriotism has vanquished their Socialism. Slaves themselves of the German Government, they fulminate against the French Government as tyrants. The only difference between Bismarck and Napoleon III was that the one was a successful and the other an unsuccessful scoundrel, one was a scoundrel, and the other a scoundrel and a half.

The German Socialists' idea of a Free State is a contradiction in terms, an unrealisable dream. Socialism implying the destruction of the State, those who support the State must renounce Socialism; must sacrifice the economic emancipation of the masses to the political power of some privileged party — and in this case it will be bourgeois democracy.

The programme of the Social Democrats really implies that they trust the bourgeois democrats to help the workers to achieve a Social revolution, after the workers have helped the bourgeois to achieve a political revolution. The way they have swallowed bourgeois ideas is shown by the list of immediate objectives, which except for the last, comprise the well-known programme of bourgeois democracy. And in fact these immediate objectives have become their real objectives, so that they have lent the Social Democratic Party to become a mere tool in the hands of the bourgeois democrats.

Does Marx himself sincerely want the antagonism of class against class, that antagonism which renders absolutely impossible any participation of the masses in the political action of the State? For this action, considered apart from the bourgeoisie, is not practicable: it is only possible when it develops in conjunction with some party of that class and lets itself be directed by the bourgeois. Marx cannot be ignorant of that, and besides, what is going on today in Geneva, Zurich, Basel, and all over Germany, ought to open his eyes on this point, if he had closed them, which, frankly, I do not believe. It is impossible for me to believe it after having read the speech he delivered recently at Amsterdam, in which he said that in certain countries, perhaps in Holland itself, the social question could be resolved peacefully, legally, without force, in a friendly fashion, which can mean nothing but this: it can be resolved by a series of successive, pacific, voluntary and judicious compromises, between bourgeoisie and proletariat. Mazzini never said anything different from that.

Mazzini and Marx are agreed on this point of capital importance, that the great social reforms which are to emancipate the proletariat cannot be realised except in a great democratic, Republican, very powerful and strongly centralised State, which for the proper well-being of the people, in order to be able to give them education and social welfare, must impose on them, by means of their own vote, a very strong government.

I maintain that if ever the Marxian party, that of so-called Social Democracy, continues to pursue the course of political demands, it will see itself forced to condemn, sooner or later, that of economic demands, the course of strike action, so incompatible are these two courses in reality.

It is always the same German temperament and the same logic which leads the Marxists directly and fatally into what we call Bourgeois Socialism and to the conclusion of a new political pact between the bourgeois who are Radicals, or who are forced to become such, and the "intelligent", respectable, that is to say, duly bourgeoisfied minority of the town proletariat to the detriment of the mass of the proletariat, not only in the country, but in the towns also.

Such is the true meaning of workers' candidatures to the Parliaments of existing States, and that of the conquest of political power by the working class. For even from the point of view of only the town proletariat to whose exclusive profit it is desired to take possession of political power, is it not clear that the popular nature of this power will never be anything else than fiction? It will be obviously impossible for some hundreds of thousands or even some tens of thousands or indeed for only a few thousand men to effectively exercise this power. They will necessarily exercise it by proxy, that is to say, entrust it to a group of men elected by themselves to represent and govern them, which will cause them without fail to fall back again into all the falsehoods and servitudes of the representative or bourgeois regime. After a brief moment of liberty or revolutionary orgy, citizens of a new State, they will awake to find themselves slaves, playthings and victims of new powerlusters. One can understand how and why clever politicians should attach themselves with great passion to a programme which opens such a wide horizon to their ambition; but that serious workers, who bear in the hearts like a living flame the sentiment of solidarity with their companions in slavery and wretchedness the whole world over, and who desire to emancipate themselves not to the detriment of all but by the emancipation of all, to be free themselves with all and not to become tyrants in their turn; that sincere toilers could become enamoured of such a programme, that is much more difficult to understand.

But then, I have a firm confidence that in a few years the German workers themselves, recognising the fatal consequences of a theory which can only favour the ambition of their bourgeois chiefs or indeed that of some exceptional workers who seek to climb on the shoulders of their comrades in order to become dominating and exploiting bourgeois in their turn—I have confidence that the German workers will reject this theory with contempt and wrath, and that they will embrace the true programme of working-class emancipation, that of the destruction of States, with as much passion as do today the workers of the great Mediterranean countries, France, Spain, Italy, as well as the Dutch and Belgian workers.

Meanwhile we recognise the perfect right of the German workers to go the way that seems to them best, provided that they allow us the same liberty. We recognise even that it is very possible that by all their history, their particular nature, the state of their civilisation and their whole situation today, they are forced to go this way. Let then the German, American and English toilers try to win political power since they desire to do so. But let them allow the toilers of other countries to march with the same energy to the destruction of all political power. Liberty for all, and a natural respect for that liberty; such are the essential conditions of international solidarity.

The German Social Democratic Labour Party founded in 1869 by Liebknecht and Bebel, under the auspices of Marx, announced in its programme that the conquest of political power was the preliminary condition of the economic emancipation of the proletariat, and that consequently the immediate object of the party must be the organisation of a widespread legal agitation for the winning of universal suffrage and of all other political rights; its final aim, the establishment of the great pan-German and so-called People's State.

Between this tendency and that of the Alliance which rejected all political action, now having as immediate and direct objective the triumph of the workers over Capitalism, and as a consequence, the abolition of the State, there exists the same difference, the same abyss, as between the proletariat and the bourgeoisie. The Alliance, taking the programme of the International seriously, had rejected contemptuously all compromise with bourgeois politics, in however Radical and Socialist a guise it might do itself up, advising the proletariat as the only way of real emancipation, as the only policy truly salutary for them, the exclusively negative policy of the demolition of political institutions, of political power, of government in general, of the State, and as a necessary consequence the international organisation of the scattered forces of the proletariat into revolutionary power directed against all the established powers of the bourgeoisie.

The Social Democrats of Germany, quite on the contrary, advised all the workers so unfortunate as to listen to them, to adopt, as the immediate objective of their association, legal agitation for the preliminary conquest of political rights; they thus subordinate the movement for economic emancipation to the movement first of all exclusively political, and by this obvious reversal of the whole programme of the International, they have filled in at a single stroke the abyss they had opened between proletariat and bourgeoisie. They have done more than that, they have tied the proletariat in tow with the bourgeoisie. For it is evident that all this political movement so boosted by the German Socialists, since it must precede the economic revolution, can only be directed by the bourgeois, or what will be still worse, by workers transformed into bourgeois by their ambition and vanity, and, passing in reality over the head of the proletariat, like all its predecessors, this movement will not fail once more to condemn the proletariat to be nothing but a blind instrument inevitably sacrificed in the struggle of the different bourgeois parties between themselves for the conquest of political power, that is to say, for the power and right to dominate the masses and exploit them. To whomsoever doubts it, we should only have to show what is happening in Germany, where the organs of Social Democracy sing hymns of joy on seeing a Congress (at Eisenach) of professors of bourgeois political economy recommending the proletariat of Germany to the high and paternal protection of States, and in the parts of Switzerland where the Marxian programme prevails, at Geneva, Zurich, Basel, where the International has descended to the point of being no longer anything more than a sort of electoral box for the profit of the Radical bourgeois. These incontestable facts seem to me to be more eloquent than any words.

They are real and logical in this sense, that they are a natural effect of the triumph of Marxian propaganda. And it is for that reason that we fight the Marxian theories to the death, convinced that if they could triumph throughout the International, they would certainly not fail to kill at least its spirit everywhere, as they have already done in very great part in the countries just mentioned.

The instinctive passion of the masses for economic equality is so great that if they could hope to receive it from the hands of despotism, they would indubitably and without much reflection do as they have often done before, and deliver themselves to despotism. Happily, historic experience has been of some service even with the masses. Today, they are beginning everywhere to understand that no despotism has, nor can have, either the will or the power to give them economic equality. The programme of the International is very happily explicit on this question. The emancipation of the toilers can be the work only of the toilers themselves.

Is it not astonishing that Marx has believed it possible to graft on this nevertheless so precise declaration, which he probably drafted himself, his scientific Socialism? That is to say, the organisation and the government of the new society by Socialistic scientists and professors—the worst of all despotic government!

But thanks to this great beloved "riff raff" of the common people, who will oppose themselves, urged on by an instinct invincible as well as just, to all the governmentalist fancies of this little working-class minority already properly disciplined and marshaled to become the myrmidons of a new despotism, the scientific Socialism of Marx will always remain as a Marxian dream. This new experience, more dismal perhaps than all past experiences, will be spared society, because the proletariat in general, and in all countries is animated today by a profound distrust against what is political and against all the politicians in the world, whatever their party colour, all of them having equally deceived, oppressed, exploited—the reddest Republicans just as much as the most absolutist Monarchists.

The Policy Of The International

I.

"Up to now we believed," says a reactionary paper, "that the political and religious opinions of a man depended upon the fact of his being a member of the International or not."

At first sight, one might think that this paper was correct in its altered opinion. For the International does not ask any new member if he is of a religious or atheistic turn of mind. She does not ask if he belongs to this or that or no political party. She simply says: Are you a worker? If not, do you feel the necessity of devoting yourself wholly to the interests of the working class, and of avoiding all movements that are opposed to it? Do you feel at one with the workers? And have you the strength in you that is requisite if you would be loyal to their cause? Are you aware that the workers—who create all wealth, who have made civilization and fought for liberty—are doomed to live in misery, ignorance, and slavery? Do you understand that the main root of all the evils that the workers experience, is poverty? And that poverty—which is the common lot of the worker—in all parts of the world—is a consequence of the present economic organization of society, and especially of the enslavement of labour—i.e. the proletariat—under the yoke of capitalism—i.e the bourgeoisie?

Do you know that between the proletariat and the bourgeoisie there exists a deadly antagonism which is the logical consequence of the economic positions of the two classes? Do you know that the wealth of the bourgeoisie is incompatible with the comfort and liberty of the workers, because their excessive wealth is, and can only be, built upon the robbing and enslavement of the workers? Do you understand that for the same reason, the prosperity and dignity of the labouring masses inevitably demands the entire abolition of the bourgeoisie? Do you realise that no single worker, however intelligent and energetic he may be, can fight successfully against the excellently organized forces of the bourgeoisie—a force which is upheld mainly by the organization of the State—all States?

Do you not see that, in order to become a power, you must unite—not with the bourgeoisie, which would be a folly and a crime, since all the bourgeoisie, so far as they belong to their class, are our deadly enemies? Nor with such workers as have deserted their own cause and have lowered themselves to beg for the benevolence of the governing class? But with honest men, who are moving, in all sincerity, towards the same goal as you? Do you understand that, against the powerful combinations formed by the privileged classes, the capitalists or possessors of the means and instruments of production and distribution, and all the states on earth—a local or national association—even if it belonged to one of the biggest countries in Europe—can never triumph? Do you not realise that, in order to fight and to vanquish this Capitalist combination, nothing less than an amalgamation of all local and national labour associations—i.e. The International Association of the Workers of all Lands—is required?

If you know and comprehend all this, come into our camp whatever else your political or religious convictions are. But if you are at one with us, and so long as you are at one with us, you will wish to pledge the whole of your being, by your every action as well as by your words, to the common cause, as a spontaneous and whole-hearted expression of that fervour of loyalty that will inevitably take possession of you. You will have to promise:

(1) To subordinate your personal and even your family interest, as well as political and religious bias and would-be activities, to the highest interest of our association, namely the struggle of Labour against Capital, the economic fight of the Proletariat against the Bourgeoisie.

(2) Never, in your personal interests, to compromise with the bourgeoisie.

(3) Never to attempt to secure a position above your fellow workers whereby you would become at once a bourgeois and an enemy of the proletariat; for the only difference between capitalists and workers is this: the former seek their welfare outside, and at the expense of, the welfare of the community, whilst the welfare of the latter is dependent on the solidarity of those who are robbed on the industrial field.

(4) To remain ever and always loyal to this principle of the solidarity of labour: for the smallest betrayal of this principle, the slightest deviation from this solidarity, is, in the eyes of the International, the greatest crime and shame with which a worker can soil himself.

II.

The founders of the International acted wisely in refusing to make philosophic or political principles the basis of their association, and preferring to have the exclusively economic struggle of Labour against Capital as the sole foundation. They were convinced that the moment a worker realised the class-struggle, the moment he — trusting to his right and the numerical strength of his class — enters the arena against capitalist robbery: that very moment, the force of circumstances and the evolution of the struggle will oblige him to recognise all the political, socialistic, and philosophic principles of the International. These principles are nothing more or less than the real expressions of the aims and objects of the working-class. The necessary and inevitable conclusion of these aims, their one underlying and supreme purpose, is the abolition — from the political as well as from the social viewpoint — of:

(1) The class-divisions existent in society, especially of those divisions imposed on society by, and in, the economic interests of the bourgeoisie.

(2) All Territorial States, Political Fatherlands, and Nations, and on the top of the historic ruins of this old world order, the establishment of the great international federation of all local and national productive groups.

From the philosophic point of view, the aims of the International are nothing less than the realisation of the eternal ideals of humanity, the welfare of man, the reign of equality, justice, and liberty on earth, making unnecessary all belief in heaven and all hopes for a better hereafter.

The great mass of the workers, crushed by their daily toil, live in ignorance and misery. Whatever the political and religious prejudices that have been forced into their heads may be, this mass is unconsciously Socialistic: instinctively, and, through the pinch of hunger and their position, more earnestly and truly Socialistic than all the "scientific" and "bourgeois Socialists" put together. They (the mass) are Socialists through all the circumstances of their material existence, whereas the latter (the "bourgeois Socialists") are only Socialistic through the circumstances of reasoning; and, in reality, the necessities of life have a greater influence over those of pure reasoning, because reasoning (or thought) is only the reflex of the continually developing life-force and not its basis.

The workers do not lack reality, the real longing for Socialist endeavour, but only the Socialist idea. Every worker, from the bottom of his heart, is longing for a really human existence, i.e., material comfort and mental development founded on justice, i.e., equality and liberty for each and every man in work. This cannot be realised in the existing political and social organization, which is founded on bare-faced robbery of the labouring masses. Consequently, every reflective worker becomes a revolutionary Socialist, since he is forced to realise that his emancipation can only be accomplished by the complete overthrow of present-day society. Either this organisation of injustice with its entire machine of oppressive laws and privileged institutions must disappear, or else the proletariat is condemned to eternal slavery.

This is the quintessence of the Socialist idea, whose germs can be found in the instinct of every serious thinking worker. Our object, therefore, is to make him conscious of what he wants, to awaken in him a clear idea that corresponds to his instincts: for the moment the class consciousness of the proletariat has lifted itself up to the level of their instinctive feeling, their intention will have developed into determination, and their power will be irresistible.

What prevents the quicker development of this idea of salvation amongst the Proletariat? Its ignorance; and, to a great extent, the political and religious prejudices with which the governing class are trying to befog the consciousness and the natural intelligence of the people. How can you disperse this ignorance and destroy these strange prejudices? "The liberation of the Proletariat must be the work of the Proletariat itself," says the preface to our general statute (The International). And it is a thousand times true! This is the main foundation of our great association. But the working class is still very ignorant. It lacks completely every theory. There is only one way out therefore, namely — Proletarian liberation through action. And what will this action be that will bring the masses to Socialism? It is the economic struggle of the Proletariat against the governing class carried out in solidarity. It is the Industrial Organisation of the workers of the world.

The Paris Commune And The Idea Of The State

This work, like all my published work, of which there has not been a great deal, is an outgrowth of events. It is the natural continuation of my Letters to a Frenchman (September 1870), wherein I had the easy but painful distinction of foreseeing and foretelling the dire calamities which now beset France and the whole civilized world, the only cure for which is the Social Revolution.

My purpose now is to prove the need for such a revolution. I shall review the historical development of society and what is now taking place in Europe, right before our eyes. Thus all those who sincerely thirst for truth can accept it and proclaim openly and unequivocally the philosophical principles and practical aims which are at the very core of what we call the Social Revolution.

I know my self-imposed task is not a simple one. I might be called presumptuous had I any personal motives in undertaking it. Let me assure my reader, I have none. I am not a scholar or a philosopher, not even a professional writer. I have not done much writing in my life and have never written except, so to speak, in self-defense, and only when a passionate conviction forced me to overcome my instinctive dislike for any public exhibition of myself.

Well, then, who am I, and what is it that prompts me to publish this work at this time? I am an impassioned seeker of the truth, and as bitter an enemy of the vicious fictions used by the established order—an order which has profited from all the religious, metaphysical, political, juridical, economic, and social infamies of all times—to brutalize and enslave the world. I am a fanatical lover of liberty. I consider it the only environment in which human intelligence, dignity, and happiness can thrive and develop. I do not mean that formal liberty which is dispensed, measured out, and regulated by the State; for this is a perennial lie and represents nothing but the privilege of a few, based upon the servitude of the remainder. Nor do I mean that individualist, egoist, base, and fraudulent liberty extolled by the school of Jean Jacques Rousseau and every other school of bourgeois liberalism, which considers the rights of all, represented by the State, as a limit for the rights of each; it always, necessarily, ends up by reducing the rights of individuals to zero. No, I mean the only liberty worthy of the name, the liberty which implies the full development of all the material, intellectual, and moral capacities latent in every one of us; the liberty which knows no other restrictions but those set by the laws of our own nature. Consequently there are, properly speaking, no restrictions, since these laws are not imposed upon us by any legislator from outside, alongside, or above ourselves. These laws are subjective, inherent in ourselves; they constitute the very basis of our being. Instead of seeking to curtail them, we should see in them the real condition and the effective cause of our liberty—that liberty of each man which does not find another man's freedom a boundary but a confirmation and vast extension of his own; liberty through solidarity, in equality. I mean liberty triumphant over brute force and, what has always been the real expression of such force, the principle of authority.

I mean liberty which will shatter all the idols in heaven and on earth and will then build a new world of mankind in solidarity upon the ruins of all the churches and all the states.

I am a convinced advocate of economic and social equality because I know that without it, liberty, justice, human dignity, morality, and the well-being of individuals, as well as the prosperity of nations, will never amount to more than a pack of lies. But since I stand for liberty as the primary condition of mankind, I believe that equality must be established in the world by the spontaneous organization of labor and the collective ownership of property by freely organized producers' associations, and by the equally spontaneous federation of communes, to replace the domineering paternalistic State.

It is at this point that a fundamental division arises between the socialists and revolutionary collectivists on the one hand and the authoritarian communists who support the absolute power of the State on the other. Their ultimate aim is identical. Both equally desire to create a new social order based first on the organization of collective labor, inevitably imposed upon each and all by the natural force of events, under conditions equal for all, and second, upon the collective ownership of the tools of production.

The difference is only that the communists imagine they can attain their goal by the development and organization of the political power of the working classes, and chiefly of the proletariat of the cities, aided by bourgeois radicalism. The revolutionary socialists, on the other hand, believe they can succeed only through the development and organization of the nonpolitical or antipolitical social power of the working classes in city and country, including all men of goodwill from the upper classes who break with their past and wish openly to join them and accept their revolutionary program in full.

This divergence leads to a difference in tactics. The communists believe it necessary to organize the workers' forces in order to seize the political power of the State. The revolutionary socialists organize for the purpose of destroying—or, to put it more politely—liquidating the State. The communists advocate the principle and the practices of authority; the revolutionary socialists put all their faith in liberty. Both equally favor science, which is to eliminate superstition and take the place of religious faith. The former would like to impose science by force; the latter would try to propagate it so that human groups, once convinced, would organize and federalize spontaneously, freely, from the bottom up, of their own accord and true to their own interests, never following a prearranged plan imposed upon "ignorant" masses by a few "superior" minds.

The revolutionary socialists hold that there is a great deal more practical good sense and wisdom in the instinctive aspirations and real needs of the masses than in the profound intelligence of all the doctors and guides of humanity who, after so many failures, still keep on trying to make men happy. The revolutionary socialists, furthermore, believe that mankind has for too long submitted to being governed; that the cause of its troubles does not lie in any particular form of government but in the fundamental principles and the very existence of government, whatever form it may take.

Finally, there is the well-known contradiction between communism as developed scientifically by the German school and accepted in part by the Americans and the English, and Proudhonism, greatly developed and taken to its ultimate conclusion by the proletariat of the Latin countries. Revolutionary socialism has just attempted its first striking and practical demonstration in the Paris Commune.

I am a supporter of the Paris Commune, which for all the bloodletting it suffered at the hands of monarchical and clerical reaction, has nonetheless grown more enduring and more powerful in the hearts and minds of Europe's proletariat. I am its supporter, above all, because it was a bold, clearly formulated negation of the State.

It is immensely significant that this rebellion against the State has taken place in France, which had been hitherto the land of political centralization par excellence, and that it was precisely Paris, the leader and the fountainhead of the great French civilization, which took the initiative in the Commune. Paris, casting aside her crown and enthusiastically proclaiming her own defeat in order to give life and liberty to France, to Europe, to the entire world; Paris reaffirming her historic power of leadership, showing to all the enslaved peoples (and are there any masses that are not slaves?) the only road to emancipation and health; Paris inflicting a mortal blow upon the political traditions of bourgeois radicalism and giving a real basis to revolutionary socialism against the reactionaries of France and Europe! Paris shrouded in her own ruins, to give the solemn lie to triumphant reaction; saving, by her own disaster, the honor and the future of France, and proving to mankind that if life, intelligence, and moral strength have departed from the upper classes, they have been preserved in their power and promises in the proletariat! Paris inaugurating the new era of the definitive and complete emancipation of the masses and their real solidarity across state frontiers; Paris destroying nationalism and erecting the religion of humanity upon its ruins; Paris proclaiming herself humanitarian and atheist, and replacing divine fictions with the great realities of social life and faith in science, replacing the lies and inequities of the old morality with the principles of liberty, justice, equality, and fraternity, those eternal bases of all human morality! Paris heroic, rational and confident, confirming her strong faith in the destinies of mankind by her own glorious downfall, her death; passing down her faith, in all its power, to the generations to come! Paris, drenched in the blood of her noblest children — this is humanity itself, crucified by the united international reaction of Europe, under the direct inspiration of all the Christian churches and that high priest of iniquity, the Pope. But the coming international revolution, expressing the solidarity of the peoples, shall be the resurrection of Paris.

This is the true meaning, and these are the immense, beneficent results of two months which encompassed the life and death of the ever memorable Paris Commune.

The Paris Commune lasted too short a time, and its internal development was too hampered by the mortal struggle it had to engage in against the Versailles reaction to allow it at least to formulate, if not apply, its socialist program theoretically. We must realize, too, that the majority of the members of the Commune were not socialists, properly speaking. If they appeared to be, it was because they were drawn in this direction by the irresistible course of events, the nature of the situation, the necessities of their position, rather than through personal conviction. The socialists were a tiny minority — there were, at most, fourteen or fifteen of them; the rest were Jacobins. But, let us make it clear, there are Jacobins and Jacobins. There are Jacobin lawyers and doctrinaires, like Mr. Gambetta; their positivist, presumptuous, despotic, and legalistic republicanism had repudiated the old revolutionary faith, leaving nothing of Jacobinism but its cult of unity and authority, and delivered the people of France over to the Prussians, and later still to native-born reactionaries. And there are Jacobins who are frankly revolutionaries, the heroes, the last sincere representatives of the democratic faith of 1793; able to sacrifice both their well-armed unity and authority rather than submit their conscience to the insolence of the reaction. These magnanimous Jacobins led naturally by Delescluze, a great soul and a great character, desire the triumph of the Revolution above everything else; and since there is no revolution without the masses, and since the masses nowadays reveal an instinct for socialism and can only make an economic and social revolution, the Jacobins of good faith, letting themselves be impelled increasingly by the logic of the revolutionary movement, will end up becoming socialists in spite of themselves.

This precisely was the situation in which the Jacobins who participated in the Paris Commune found themselves. Delescluze, and many others with him, signed programs and proclamations whose general import and promise were of a positively socialist nature. However, in spite of their good faith and all their goodwill, they were merely socialists impelled by outward circumstances rather than by an inward conviction;

they lacked the time and even the capacity to overcome and subdue many of their own bourgeois prejudices which were contrary to their newly acquired socialism. One can understand that, trapped in this internal struggle, they could never go beyond generalities or take any of those decisive measures that would end their solidarity and all their contacts with the bourgeois world forever.

This was a great misfortune for the Commune and these men. They were paralyzed, and they paralyzed the Commune. Yet we cannot blame them. Men are not transformed overnight; they do not change their natures or their habits at will. They proved their sincerity by letting themselves be killed for the Commune. Who would dare ask more of them?

They are no more to be blamed than the people of Paris, under whose influence they thought and acted. The people were socialists more by instinct than by reflection. All their aspirations are in the highest degree socialist but their ideas, or rather their traditional expressions, are not. The proletariat of the great cities of France, and even of Paris, still cling to many Jacobin prejudices, and to many dictatorial and governmental concepts. The cult of authority—the fatal result of religious education, that historic source of all evils, depravations, and servitude—has not yet been completely eradicated in them. This is so true that even the most intelligent children of the people, the most convinced socialists, have not freed themselves completely of these ideas. If you rummage around a bit in their minds, you will find the Jacobin, the advocate of government, cowering in a dark corner, humble but not quite dead.

And, too, the small group of convinced socialists who participated in the Commune were in a very difficult position. While they felt the lack of support from the great masses of the people of Paris, and while the organization of the International Association, itself imperfect, compromised hardly a few thousand persons, they had to keep up a daily struggle against the Jacobin majority. In the midst of the conflict, they had to feed and provide work for several thousand workers, organize and arm them, and keep a sharp lookout for the doings of the reactionaries. All this in an immense city like Paris, besieged, facing the threat of starvation, and a prey to all the shady intrigues of the reaction, which managed to establish itself in Versailles with the permission and by the grace of the Prussians. They had to set up a revolutionary government and army against the government and army of Versailles; in order to fight the monarchist and clerical reaction they were compelled to organize themselves in a Jacobin manner, forgetting or sacrificing the first conditions of revolutionary socialism.

In this confusing situation, it was natural that the Jacobins, the strongest section, constituting the majority of the Commune, who also possessed a highly developed political instinct, the tradition and practice of governmental organization, should have had the upper hand over the socialists. It is a matter of surprise that they did not press their advantage more than they did; that they did not give a fully Jacobin character to the Paris insurrection; that, on the contrary, they let themselves be carried along into a social revolution.

I know that many socialists, very logical in their theory, blame our Paris friends for not having acted sufficiently as socialists in their revolutionary practice. The yelping pack of the bourgeois press, on the other hand, accuse them of having followed their program too faithfully. Let us forget, for a moment, the ignoble denunciations of that press. I want to call the attention of the strictest theoreticians of proletarian emancipation to the fact that they are unjust to our Paris brothers, for between the most correct theories and their practical application lies an enormous distance which cannot be bridged in a few days. Whoever had the pleasure of knowing Varlin, for instance (to name just one man whose death is certain), knows that he and his friends were guided by profound, passionate, and well-considered socialist convictions. These were men whose ardent zeal, devotion, and good faith had never been questioned by those who had known them. Yet, precisely because they were men of good faith, they were filled with self-distrust in the face of the immense task to which they had devoted their minds and their lives; they thought too little of themselves! And they were convinced that in the Social Revolution, diametrically opposite to a political revolution in this as in other ways, individual action was to be almost nil, while the spontaneous action of the masses had to be everything. All that individuals can do is formulate, clarify, and propagate ideas expressing the instinctive desires of the people, and contribute their constant efforts to the revolutionary organization of the natural powers of the masses. This and nothing more; all the rest can be accomplished only by the people themselves. Otherwise we would end up with a political dictatorship—the reconstitution of the State, with all its privileges, inequalities, and oppressions; by taking a devious but inevitable path we would come to reestablish the political, social, and economic slavery of the masses.

Varlin and all his friends, like all sincere socialists, and generally like all workers born and bred among the people, shared this perfectly legitimate feeling of caution toward the continuous activity of one and the same group of individuals and against the domination exerted by superior personalities. And since they were just and fair-minded men above all else, they turned this foresight, this mistrust, against themselves as much as against other persons.

Contrary to the belief of authoritarian communists—which I deem completely wrong—that a social revolution must be decreed and organized either by a dictatorship or by a constituent assembly emerging from a political revolution, our friends, the Paris socialists, believed that revolution could neither be made nor brought to its full development except by the spontaneous and continued action of the masses, the groups and the associations of the people.

Our Paris friends were right a thousand times over. In fact, where is the mind, brilliant as it may be, or—if we speak of a collective dictatorship, even if it were formed of several hundred individuals endowed with superior mentalities—

where are the intellects powerful enough to embrace the infinite multiplicity and diversity of real interests, aspirations, wishes and needs which sum up the collective will of the people? And to invent a social organization that will not be a Procrustean bed upon which the violence of the State will more or less overtly force unhappy society to stretch out? It has always been thus, and it is exactly this old system of organization by force that the Social Revolution should end by granting full liberty to the masses, the groups, the communes, the associations and to the individuals as well; by destroying once and for all the historic cause of all violence, which is the power and indeed the mere existence of the State. Its fall will bring down with it all the inequities of the law and all the lies of the various religions, since both law and religion have never been anything but the compulsory consecration, ideal and real, of all violence represented, guaranteed, and protected by the State.

It is obvious that liberty will never be given to humanity, and that the real interests of society, of all groups, local associations, and individuals who make up society will never be satisfied until there are no longer any states. It is obvious that all the so-called general interests of society, which the State is supposed to represent and which are in reality just a general and constant negation of the true interests of regions, communes, associations, and individuals subject to the State, are a mere abstraction, a fiction, a lie. The State is like a vast slaughterhouse or an enormous cemetery, where all the real aspirations, all the living forces of a country enter generously and happily, in the shadow of that abstraction, to let themselves be slain and buried. And just as no abstraction exists for and by itself, having no legs to sand on, no arms to create with, no stomach to digest the mass of victims delivered to it, it is likewise clear that the celestial or religious abstraction, God, actually represents the very real interests of a class, the clergy, while its terrestrial complement, that political abstraction, the State, represents the no less real interests of the exploiting class which tends to absorb all the others—the bourgeoisie. As the clergy has always been divisive, and nowadays tends to separate men even further into a very powerful and wealthy minority and a sad and rather wretched majority, so likewise the bourgeoisie, with its various social and political organizations in industry, agriculture, banking, and commerce, as well as in all administrative, financial, judiciary, education, police, and military functions of the State tend increasingly to weld all of these into a really dominant oligarchy on the one hand, and on the other hand into an enormous mass of more or less hopeless creatures, defrauded creatures who live in a perpetual illusion, steadily and inevitably pushed down into the proletariat by the irresistible force of the present economic development, and reduced to serving as blind tools of this all-powerful oligarchy.

The abolition of the Church and the State should be the first and indispensable condition for the real enfranchisement of society, which can and should reorganize itself not from the top down according to an ideal plan dressed up by wise men or scholars nor by decrees promulgated by some dictatorial power or even by a national assembly elected through universal suffrage. Such a system, as I have already said, would inevitably lead to the creation of a new state and, consequently, to the formation of a ruling aristocracy, that is, an entire class of persons who have nothing in common with the masses. And, of course, this class would exploit and subject the masses, under the pretext of serving the common welfare or saving the State.

The future social organization should be carried out from the bottom up, by the free association or federation of workers, starting with the associations, then going on to the communes, the regions, the nations, and, finally, culminating in a great international and universal federation. It is only then that the true, life-giving social order of liberty and general welfare will come into being, a social order which, far from restricting, will affirm and reconcile the interests of individuals and of society.

It is said that the harmony and universal solidarity of individuals with society can never be attained in practice because their interests, being antagonistic, can never be reconciled. To this objection I reply that if these interest have never as yet come to mutual accord, it was because the State has sacrificed the interests of the majority for the benefit of a privileged minority. That is why this famous incompatibility, this conflict of personal interests with those of society, is nothing but a fraud, a political lie, born of the theological lie which invented the doctrine of original sin in order to dishonor man and destroy his self-respect. The same false idea concerning irreconcilable interests was also fostered by the dreams of metaphysics which, as we know, is close kin to theology. Metaphysics, failing to recognize the social character of human nature, looked upon society as a mechanical and purely artificial aggregate of individuals, suddenly brought together in the name of some formal or secret compact concluded freely or under the influence of a superior power. Before uniting in society, these individuals, endowed with some sort of immortal soul, enjoyed complete liberty, according to the metaphysicians. We are convinced that all the wealth of man's intellectual, moral, and material development, as well as his apparent independence, is the product of his life in society. Outside society, not only would he not be a free man, he would not even become genuinely human, a being conscious of himself, the only being who thinks and speaks. Only the combination of intelligence and collective labor was able to force man out of that savage and brutish state which constituted his original nature, or rather the starting point for his further development. We are profoundly convinced that the entire life of men—their interests, tendencies, needs, illusions, even stupidities, as well as very bit of violence, injustice, and seemingly voluntary activity—merely represent the result of inevitable societal forces. People cannot reject the idea of mutual independence, nor can they deny the reciprocal influence and uniformity exhibiting the manifestations of external nature.

In nature herself, this marvelous correlation and interdependence of phenomena certainly is not produced without struggle. On the contrary, the harmony of the forces of nature appears only as the result of a continual struggle, which is the real condition of life and of movement. In nature, as in society, order without struggle is death.

If order is natural and possible in the universe, it is only because the universe is not governed according to some pre imagined system imposed by a supreme will. The theological hypothesis of divine legislation leads to an obvious absurdity, to the negation not only of all order but of nature herself. Natural laws are real only in that they are inherent in nature; that is, they are not established by any authority. These laws are but simple manifestations, or rather continuous variations, of the uniformities constituting what we call "nature." Human intelligence and its science have observed them, have checked them experimentally, assembled them into a system and called them laws. But nature as such knows no laws. She acts unconsciously; she represents in herself the infinite variety of phenomena which appear and repeat themselves inevitably. This inevitability of action is the reason the universal order can and does exist.

Such an order is also apparent in human society, which seems to have evolved in an allegedly anti-natural way but actually is determined by the natural animal's needs and his capacity for thinking that have contributed a special element to his development — a completely natural element, by the way, in the sense that men, like everything that exists, represent the material product of the union and action of natural forces. This special element is reason, the captivity for generalization and abstraction, thanks to which man is able to project himself in his thought, examining and observing himself like a strange, eternal object. By lifting himself in thought above himself, and above the world around him, he reaches the representation of perfect abstraction, the absolute void. And this absolute is nothing less than his capacity for abstraction, which disdains all that exists and finds its repose in attaining complete negation. This is the ultimate limit of the highest abstraction of the mind; this absolute nothingness is God.

This is the meaning and the historical foundation of every theological doctrine. As they did not understand the nature and the material causes of their own thinking, and did not even grasp the conditions or natural laws underlying such thinking, these early men and early societies had not the slightest suspicion that their absolute notions were simply the result of their own capacity for formulating abstract ideas. Hence they viewed these ideas, drawn from nature, as real objects, next to which nature herself ceased to amount to anything. They began to worship their fictions, their improbable notions of the absolute, and to honor them. But since they felt the need of giving some concrete form to the abstract idea of nothingness or of God, they created the concept of divinity and, furthermore, endowed it with all the qualities and powers, good and evil, which they found only in nature and in society. Such was the origin and historical development of all religions, from fetishism on down to Christianity.

We do not intend to undertake a study of the history of religious, theological, and metaphysical absurdities or to discuss the procession of all the divine incarnations and visions created by centuries of barbarism. We all know that superstition brought disaster and caused rivers of blood and tears to flow. All these revolting aberrations of poor mankind were historical, inevitable stages in the normal growth and evolution of social organizations. Such aberrations engendered the fatal idea which dominated men's imagination, that the universe was governed by a supernatural power and will. Centuries came and went, and societies grew accustomed to this idea to such an extent that they finally destroyed any urge toward or capacity to achieve further progress which arose in their midst.

The lust for power of a few individuals originally, and of several social classes later, established slavery and conquest as the dominant principle, and implanted this terrible idea of divinity in the heart of society. Thereafter no society was viewed as feasible without these two institutions, the Church and the State, at its base. These two social scourges are defended by all their doctrinaire apologists.

No sooner did these institutions appear in the world than two ruling classes—the priests and the aristocrats—promptly organized themselves and lost no time in indoctrinating the enslaved people with the idea of the utility, indispensability, and sacredness of the Church and of the State.

CPSIA information can be obtained
at www.ICGtesting.com
Printed in the USA
LVHW051322030621
689199LV00014B/885

9 781934 941836